SCRATCH PROGRAMMING
PLAYGROUND

SCRATCH PROGRAMMING PLAYGROUND

LEARN TO PROGRAM BY MAKING COOL GAMES

BY AL SWEIGART

no starch
press

San Francisco

SCRATCH PROGRAMMING PLAYGROUND. Copyright © 2016 by Al Sweigart.

Printed in USA

Second printing

20 19 18 17   2 3 4 5 6 7 8 9

ISBN-10: 1-59327-762-8
ISBN-13: 978-1-59327-762-8

Publisher: William Pollock
Production Editor: Laurel Chun
Cover Illustration: Josh Ellingson
Illustrator: Miran Lipovača
Interior Design: Beth Middleworth
Developmental Editor: Tyler Ortman
Technical Reviewer: Martin Tan
Copyeditor: Anne Marie Walker
Compositor: Laurel Chun
Proofreader: Lisa Devoto-Farrell

For information on distribution, translations, or bulk sales, please contact No Starch Press, Inc. directly:
No Starch Press, Inc.
245 8th Street, San Francisco, CA 94103
phone: 1.415.863.9900; info@nostarch.com
www.nostarch.com

Library of Congress Cataloging-in-Publication Data

```
Names: Sweigart, Al, author.
Title: Scratch programming playground : learn to program by making cool games
   / Al Sweigart.
Description: San Francisco : No Starch Press, [2016] | Audience: Ages 8+. |
   Includes index.
Identifiers: LCCN 2016022304 (print) | LCCN 2016024406 (ebook) | ISBN
   9781593277628 | ISBN 1593277628 | ISBN 9781593277963 (epub) | ISBN
   1593277962 (epub) | ISBN 9781593277970 ( mobi) | ISBN 1593277970 (mobi)
Subjects: LCSH: Scratch (Computer program language)--Juvenile literature. |
   Computer games--Programming--Juvenile literature. | Computer
   programming--Juvenile literature. | Microcomputers--Programming--Juvenile
   literature.
Classification: LCC QA76.73.S345 S94 2016 (print) | LCC QA76.73.S345 (ebook)
   | DDC 005.13/3--dc23
LC record available at https://lccn.loc.gov/2016022304
```

For Seymour Papert,
So long and thanks for all the turtles
(February 29, 1928 – July 31, 2016)

ABOUT THE AUTHOR

Al Sweigart is a software developer, tech book author, and hoopy frood who really knows where his towel is. He has written several programming books for beginners, including *Automate the Boring Stuff with Python*, also from No Starch Press. His books are freely available under a Creative Commons license at his website *http://www.inventwithpython.com/*.

ABOUT THE TECHNICAL REVIEWER

Martin Tan helps run a Code Club in Australia, and he wrote the space-themed Scratch and Python projects for Moonhack 2016 that brought over 9,000 kids together to break the world record for children coding simultaneously. Martin also works as a penetration tester, contributing to various open source projects and research.

BRIEF CONTENTS

CONTENTS IN DETAIL

3
MAZE RUNNER   35

ACKNOWLEDGMENTS

It's misleading to have just my name on the cover. This book wouldn't exist without the efforts of many people. I'd like to thank my publisher, Bill Pollock; my editors, Laurel Chun and Tyler Ortman; my technical reviewer, Martin Tan; my copy-editor, Anne Marie Walker; and all of the staff at No Starch Press.

Thanks to the MIT Media Lab's Lifelong Kindergarten group for their development of Scratch, which has a long chain of influential thinkers: Mitchel Resnick, Seymour Papert, Marvin Minsky, and Jean Piaget. While we give the younger generation a ride on our shoulders, let's never forget where we ourselves stand.

Special thanks to the Museum of Art and Digital Entertainment in Oakland, California. A video game museum is as fun to be involved with as it sounds, and volunteering with MADE's weekend Scratch class has been thoroughly rewarding. If Alex Handy, Mike Pavone, and William Morgan hadn't started the Scratch class, I never would've come up with the idea for this book. I'll see y'all next Saturday.

INTRODUCTION

P laying video games is fun, but programming your own video games is a creative,
challenging skill that will let you make
your own fun. The free Scratch programming
environment gives everyone an easy way to learn
programming skills. While Scratch is primarily
designed for 8- to 16-year-olds, it's used by people
of all ages, including younger children with their
parents and college students learning their first
programming language.

There's so much that you can do with Scratch, it's hard to know where to start. That's where this book comes in. This book guides you through creating several video games in Scratch. By building the projects in this book, you'll get a good idea of which blocks are commonly used to create video games in Scratch. These projects provide a solid foundation for you to build upon when creating your own original programs.

WHO THIS BOOK IS FOR

No previous programming experience is necessary to read this book. The only mathematics skills required are basic arithmetic: addition, subtraction, multiplication, and division. Don't let math phobia prevent you from learning to program. And don't forget that the computer will perform calculations for you!

Each program in the book is easy to make by following the step-by-step instructions. You'll learn about the code blocks and programming concepts as you make games that use them. No matter your skill level, there's no reason you can't start reading this book now!

Kids can follow along with the activities on their own, but this book is also for parents, teachers, and volunteers who want to introduce their children or students to the world of programming. The projects are ideal for a weekend activity or afterschool computer club. Adults don't have to be software engineers to use this book to help others learn.

If you want a thorough guide to all of Scratch's features, I recommend the book *Learn to Program with Scratch* by Majed Marji (No Starch Press, 2014) to supplement this one. You can also watch video tutorials online at *https:// scratch.mit.edu/help/videos/* and *https:// inventwithscratch.com/*.

But programming is a *hands-on* skill like karate or guitar: you can't learn it by reading alone! Make sure you're following along and creating the games—you'll learn a lot more that way.

ABOUT THIS BOOK

Each chapter walks you through programming a single game, and programming concepts are explained as they come up. You'll start by sketching out what the final game will look like and planning the main parts of the parts of the program. The sections that follow will cover how to code each of these parts step-by-step until you've built the full game. After building the main game, you'll have the option of adding special features and cheat modes. Review questions at the end of each chapter help you check whether you understand the topics covered.

▶ **Chapter 1: Getting Started with Scratch** shows you how to access the Scratch website and the different parts of the Scratch editor.

▶ In **Chapter 2: Rainbow Lines in Space!**, you'll create an animated art project using basic code blocks and several sprites working together. You'll also learn about directions and degrees.

▶ In **Chapter 3: Maze Runner**, you'll make a maze game in which the player uses the keyboard to change the cat's coordinates and guide it through eight different maze levels.

▶ **Chapter 4: Shooting Hoops with Gravity** shows you how to make a basketball game that implements realistic gravity for jumping cats and falling basketballs.

▶ **Chapter 5: A Polished Brick Breaker Game** covers simple techniques for taking a plain brick breaker game and turning it into a polished, exciting game with animations, sound effects, and more.

▶ **Chapter 6: Snaaaaaake!** features the classic computer game in which the player guides an ever-growing snake around the screen. It explains how to use Scratch's sprite cloning feature to make the stretching snake body.

▶ In **Chapter 7: Fruit Slicer**, you'll make a clone of the hit smartphone game *Fruit Ninja*, in which the player slices fruit in mid-air.

▶ **Chapter 8: Asteroid Breaker . . . in Space!** features a clone of the classic space shooter *Asteroids.* You'll add mouse and keyboard controls to the spaceship.

▶ Pulling together many of the concepts used in previous chapters, **Chapter 9: Making an Advanced Platformer** explains how to create a platformer game with walking and jumping animations, platforms, and AI-controlled enemies.

HOW TO USE THIS BOOK

All of the book's projects start with a sketch of the game we'll make. The labels on the sketch point to features that we'll add to the game with code.

To keeps things manageable, we'll tackle each part of the game one at a time. The blue ABC headings in the book correspond to these features in the sketch.

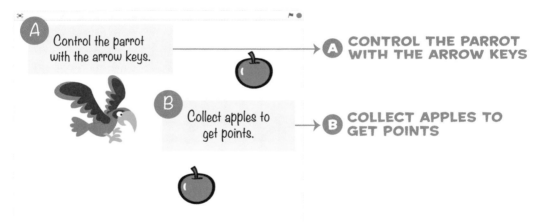

Splitting a big problem into a bunch of little problems can really help organize your thinking and make a big problem feel approachable. After we get a simple version of the game up and running, we'll add new features, cheat codes, and more. When you're ready to start creating games yourself, I recommend starting with a simple sketch.

SAVE POINT

Throughout this book you'll see these Save Point boxes. Because you'll be making programs step-by-step, you'll want to pause and run the program every so often, even if it isn't finished. You'll be able to see whether the program is working correctly so far and catch any mistakes early. The Save Point boxes will also remind you to save the program by selecting **File ▶ Save Now** in the menu bar.

ONLINE RESOURCES

Although the Scratch environment includes many images, you'll need some extra files to make the projects in this book. These files are in the resources ZIP file, which you can download from *https://www .nostarch.com/scratchplayground/*. You'll need to unzip the files to your hard drive to access them.

The resources ZIP file contains the image files used in the book's projects and the skeleton project files for each of the programs. These skeleton project files have all the setup steps already completed and only require you to add the code blocks. If you are having trouble finishing your program, you can try starting from the skeleton project file instead of a brand new, blank project. Using the skeleton project files may be a good idea if you are a teacher who is coaching several students and time is limited, because they'll only have to add the code blocks to complete the program.

ERRATA AND UPDATES

While we've done our best to keep this book error free, corrections and updates for this book will be listed at *https:// nostarch.com/scratchplayground/*.

1

GETTING STARTED
WITH SCRATCH

Scratch is the best educational programming software available today. No other
tool makes programming as easy as
Scratch does. Many similar products have been
inspired by Scratch, but Scratch remains the most
popular. With Scratch, you can create interactive
games, animations, and science projects, all while
having lots of fun!

Scratch is a free programming environment that runs in your web browser. It was designed by the MIT Media Lab's Lifelong Kindergarten Group. Scratch users, called *Scratchers*, can create programs by snapping together code blocks in the Scratch editor. Although Scratch was designed for 8- to 16-year-olds, Scratchers consist of people of all ages, including younger children with their parents. The software makes it easy for anyone to start developing their programming and problem-solving skills.

Because Scratch runs in your web browser, there's no software to install. It's impossible for a Scratch program to damage the files on your computer. Scratch is completely free—there are no ads or in-app purchases, so kids can play with everything on the Scratch site and adults don't have to worry about accidental charges.

In Scratch, you use the mouse to drag and drop code blocks, so little typing is needed. Here's an example of the snap-together code blocks:

```
when 🏳 clicked
say Hello!
forever
    move 10 steps
    turn ↺ 15 degrees
```

The visual Scratch editor provides you with quick feedback, so you don't have to type mysterious commands for hours before you can see your programs come to life. Scratch makes programming immediate and fun. And unlike other programming languages, Scratch doesn't have any error messages that pop up and confuse the programmer. If you want to learn the basics of programming (or help someone else learn), Scratch is second to none.

RUNNING SCRATCH

To start using Scratch, open your web browser and go to
https://scratch.mit.edu/. It doesn't matter whether you're running Windows, OS X, or Linux, but you do have to run Scratch
on a laptop or desktop computer. Scratch doesn't work on tab-
lets or smartphones.

NOTE   *The Raspberry Pi computer cannot run
Scratch 2.0, the version of Scratch covered in this book.*

Signing up for an account is free. You can create Scratch
programs without an account, but having the Scratch account
lets you save your programs online. Then you can continue
working on them later from any computer connected to the
internet.

Click the **Join Scratch** link at the top of the page to
create an account. A new window opens:

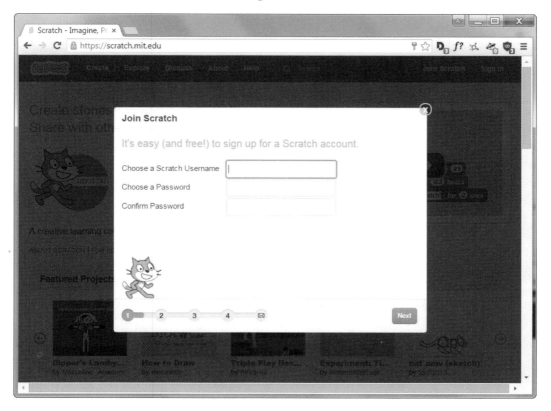

Choose a username and password, and enter your account information. Scratch will never share your email address or personal information without your permission. Its full privacy policy is at *https://scratch.mit.edu/privacy_policy/.*

After you've logged in to the Scratch website, click the **Create** link at the top of the page to start the Scratch editor.

THE OFFLINE EDITOR

The offline editor lets you program without being connected to the internet. If you don't have internet access or if your Wi-Fi is unreliable, you can install the offline editor on your computer instead of using the Scratch website. The only difference is that programs will be saved on your computer instead of on the Scratch website. You can later upload your Scratch programs or copy them to a flash drive to move them to another computer.

The Scratch offline editor is available at *https://scratch .mit.edu/scratch2download/.*

NOTE   *You may find the editor software for an earlier version, Scratch 1.4. Don't use this version; it's out-of-date and doesn't have the new features that Scratch 2.0 has. If you're using Scratch in your web browser, you're using Scratch 2.0. If you download an offline Scratch editor, be sure to download Scratch 2.0.*

THE SCRATCH EDITOR AND SPRITES

The Scratch editor is where you snap code blocks together to create your game, animation, or artwork. The **Create** link at the top of the page opens the editor, as shown in the following figure, so you can start making Scratch programs.

The most basic object in Scratch is the sprite. Sprites appear on the Stage ❻, and their code blocks control their behavior. The editor automatically starts with a cat sprite for all new projects, but you can add more sprites. You can program a sprite by adding code blocks to the Scripts Area ❺ on the right side of the screen. In Scratch, a stack of code blocks is called a *script*.

The text field at the top of the editor contains the project name ❹. After you've named your project using a descriptive name, remember to occasionally save your project by clicking **File ▶ Save Now** from the menu bar ❶ to avoid losing your work if your browser crashes.

You access the code blocks from the Blocks Area ❼ in the center. At the top of the Blocks Area are 10 categories of code blocks: *Motion, Looks, Sound, Pen, Data, Events, Control,*

Sensing, *Operators*, and *More Blocks*. Every code block belongs to one category and is the color of that category. For example, the **say** block comes from the purple *Looks* category. An infinite supply of code blocks is available; just drag them from the Blocks Area to the Scripts Area.

Each sprite has its own scripts. When you click the sprite in the Sprite List ❽, that sprite's scripts will display in the Scripts Area. Select the Scripts tab ❸ to display the Scripts Area. The Scripts Area is replaced by the Paint Editor and Sound Editor when the Costumes and Sounds tabs are selected, respectively.

Clicking the green flag will start your program, and clicking the red stop sign will stop it ❷.

THE PAINT EDITOR

There are a few ways to get sprites into your programs. You can use the sprites that come with Scratch, upload sprites from your computer, or draw your own. If you want to draw your own, you can use Scratch's Paint Editor.

The Paint Editor is similar to other painting programs, such as Microsoft Paint or Paintbrush. To draw a new sprite, click the **Paintbrush** button next to New sprite. You can change how sprites look by switching to one of many costumes. To create a new costume for a sprite, click the **Costumes** tab, and then click the **Paintbrush** button next to New Costume.

The main parts of the Paint Editor are

▶ The drawing tools, which you can select using the buttons on the left side

▶ The Canvas, where you draw images

- ▶ The Costume center, which indicates the center of the costume with the crosshairs symbol
- ▶ The Line width slider, which sets the width of the drawing tools
- ▶ The Color selector, which changes the color of the drawing tools
- ▶ The Zoom buttons for zooming into or out of the canvas
- ▶ The Undo and Redo buttons, which can help you correct mistakes

The Paint Editor looks like this:

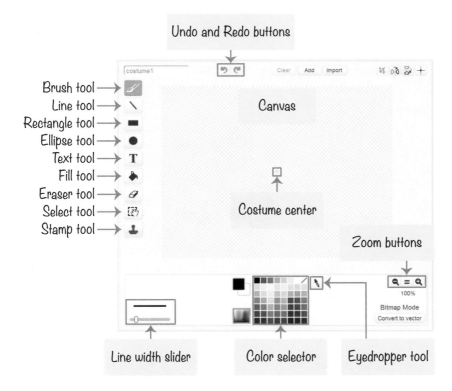

Experiment with the Paint Editor by clicking the drawing tool buttons and dragging the mouse over the Canvas to see how the tools work. Change the color and width of the drawing tools with the Color selector and Line width slider. Then use the Eyedropper tool to select a color from the Canvas rather than picking a color from the Color selector. If you make a mistake, click the Undo button at the top.

The list of sprite costumes is in the column to the left of the drawing tools. If you want to save a costume as an image file, right-click the costume and select **Save to local file**.

WORKING WITH CODE BLOCKS

Before you begin programming, it's good to get an idea of how the code blocks snap together in the editor. Throughout this book, you'll learn what each code block does.

Adding Blocks

To create a new code block, drag it from the center Blocks Area to the Scripts Area. The code blocks that have a notch on top and bump on the bottom are called *stack* blocks. To snap a stack block together with another stack block, drag the block close to the bottom of the other. When a white outline appears, drop the block to connect it to the stack.

Stack blocks can also fit in between blocks. Look carefully at where the white outline appears in the script: this is where the block will snap into place. This figure shows a **wait 1 secs** block being moved into the middle of a script:

You can change a white field inside a block by clicking the white area and entering new input. The rectangular white fields accept text; the rounded white fields accept numbers.

The rounded blocks are called *reporter* blocks. They fit inside the white fields. For example, in the following figure, the green **pick random 1 to 10** block fits inside the white field. When the *left edge* of the reporter block is over the white field, a white outline appears around the white field. If the left edge isn't over the white field, the white outline won't appear and the reporter block cannot be placed inside.

Deleting Blocks

To remove blocks, drag them out of the script. If you remove a stack block, you'll also remove the stack blocks connected under it, as shown in the next figure. You may need to set aside these blocks if you want to reconnect some of them to the script. Drag the blocks you want to delete over the center Blocks Area to remove them from the Stage. You can always add more blocks from the Blocks Area when you need them.

You can also right-click a block and select **delete** from the menu that appears. However, doing so will also delete all the blocks underneath that block. If you accidentally delete some blocks, you can restore them by selecting **Edit ▶ Undelete** from the menu bar.

Running Programs

Create the following program by dragging blocks from the Blocks Area to the Scripts Area:

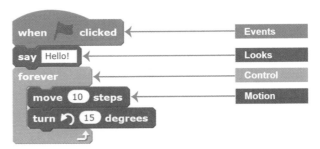

When you click the green flag at the top of the Stage, this program will start. Programs begin at the top block (**when green flag clicked**) and then run the next code block in the script. In this example, a speech bubble appears above the sprite and displays the word "Hello!" In the **forever** loop, the sprite moves forward 10 steps and then turns counterclockwise by 15 degrees. When the program gets to the last block, it *loops* back to the top. All the blocks in the **forever** block will run in a loop forever. The program stops only when you click the red stop sign.

You can also run a script or block by double-clicking it. But clicking the green flag is the normal way to start your program.

You can have as many sprites and code blocks in your programs as you want. As you create the programming projects in this book, you'll learn about Scratch's many different types of code blocks.

SHOWING OFF YOUR PROGRAMS

When you're logged in to your Scratch account, click the **Share** button at the top-right corner of the editor to let other Scratchers see your program. They'll be able to play your game and leave comments. If Scratchers enjoy playing the game, they can Like and Favorite your program.

Once you've finished a project, you can also add it to the *Scratch Programming Playground* studio. This studio features projects and remixes you and other readers have made. Once you've shared your project in Scratch, copy the URL and go to the studio's page at *https://inventwithscratch .com/studio/*. Click the **Add Projects** button, paste the URL into the text field, and click **Add by URL**. Now other readers will be able to view your game in the studio!

Don't worry if you think your game isn't good enough. Everyone begins their coding journey with simple games. Most people on the Scratch website are beginners, too. Over 11 million people have shared their programs on the Scratch website, so don't fret if yours doesn't get many views. Games can be difficult to find with so many available on the site!

GETTING HELP

Becoming a super programmer isn't about knowing all the answers; it's knowing how to find answers. You can follow the steps for the projects in this book, but you might have questions of your own.

The Tips Window

The first place to look for help is in the Scratch editor's Help section. Click the **Question mark** button on the right side of the editor to open the Tips window.

Click the Question mark button to open the Tips window.

In the Tips window, you can learn what a particular code block does by selecting it from the Blocks tab, as shown here:

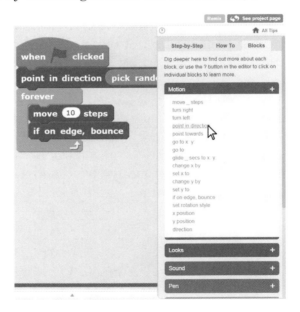

You can also access and read through several tutorials. Although you can ask for help in the discussion forums, it's faster to find answers in the Tips window.

The See Inside Button

You can learn many new techniques by looking at other Scratchers' code. Find a project you like on the Scratch website, and then click the **See inside** button, as shown here:

Click the See inside button to view other Scratchers' code.

You're allowed to copy and modify, or *remix*, other Scratchers' code. All Scratch programs on the website are automatically released under a Creative Commons license, so you don't need to ask the original creator for permission, as long as you give them credit. Scratchers often remix each other's programs to create their own versions.

Still need help and want to talk to other Scratchers? Click the **Discuss** link at the top of the website to visit the discussion forums.

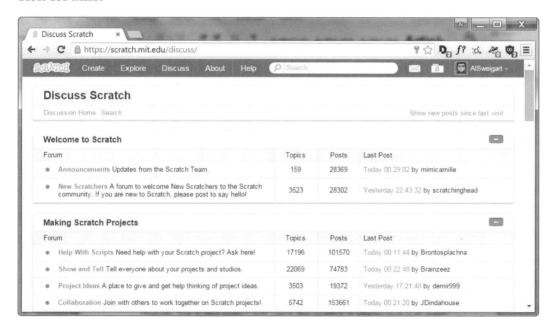

SUMMARY

The Scratch editor is a creative tool with great potential. You'll see all sorts of Scratch projects on the Scratch website: games, cartoons, simulations, and informative presentation slides.

Now that you know how to access the Scratch website, create an account, use the Scratch and Paint editors, and snap together code blocks into scripts, you're ready to follow the step-by-step instructions in the rest of this book. If you have questions, be sure to use the Tips window in the Scratch editor and the discussion forums on the Scratch website to find the answers you need.

Let's start creating your first Scratch program!

n this chapter, you'll create a cool-looking animation: a rainbow *V* that flies through space and leaves colorful trails behind. This program was inspired by the *demoscene*, a subculture of elite programmers who made amazing graphical programs starting in the 1980s.

Demosceners made beautiful, elaborate programs called *demos* that showed off their artistic, musical, and programming skills. But most amazing of all, these programs were *tiny*—just a few kilobytes! The program we'll write isn't quite as small, but it's dramatic and colorful, and it uses only a few lines of Scratch code.

Before you start coding, look at the following figure to see what the final program will look like. Then go to *https://www.nostarch.com/scratchplayground/* to play the animation.

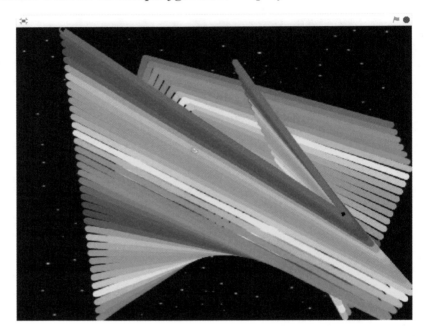

Just like demosceners, you can make beautiful programs. Let's create our own graphics demo in Scratch!

SKETCH OUT THE DESIGN

The first step of turning an idea into a Scratch program is to sketch out what you want it to look like. Planning your program helps you figure out the sprites you want and how they'll behave. I recommend drawing your ideas on paper so you can cross them out if you don't like them and write down notes and reminders.

It's also best to keep the project simple. If you start by making a complicated game like *Minecraft* or *Zelda*, you'll quickly realize that it's a lot of work. It's more rewarding to finish a small project than to deal with the frustration of an unending, unfinished, and unplayable game.

When you've completed your simple game, you can then build on top of it to make it more complex, which is the idea behind *iterative development*. First, you make the program work. Then, you make the program better. You can always add cool elements to the basic program after you finish it. Or, if your program becomes too complicated, you can return to your sketches and figure out what you want to remove.

Don't worry about making the sketch look nice. It's more important to have a solid plan for the main parts of the program. In my sketch, I have three parts: A, B, and C. We will work on these parts one at a time until we've built the full program.

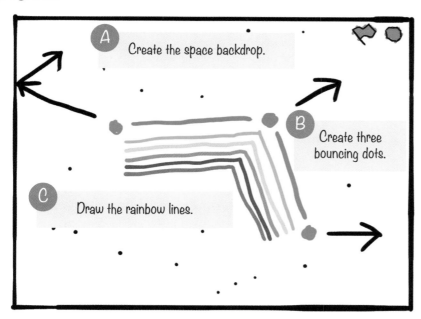

After you've completed a sketch of what you want your program to do, you can start programming! Go to *https:// scratch.mit.edu/*, sign up for an account on the site, and log in (having an account lets you save your programs on the Scratch website). After you've logged in, click the **Create** button at the top of your screen to start making your own Scratch project. Then click the text field in the top left to change the name of the project from *Untitled* to *Rainbow Lines*. Let's begin by tackling Part A of the sketch.

Ⓐ CREATE THE SPACE BACKDROP

First, let's clean up sprites we won't use and set a background.

1. Clean Up and Set the Stage

Every time you create a new Scratch project, you'll see an orange cat sprite on a blank, white Stage. We don't need the cat sprite for our program, so right-click the Sprite1 cat in the Sprite List, and select **delete** to remove the cat from the Stage and the Sprite List.

Click the **Choose backdrop from library** button (which looks like a landscape painting) under New backdrop.

The Backdrop Library window will open and display all the backdrops in alphabetical order. Select the **stars** backdrop and click **OK**.

Now the Stage's backdrop looks like outer space!

Ⓑ CREATE THREE BOUNCING DOTS

Next, we'll add three new sprites that represent the three points of the flying *V*.

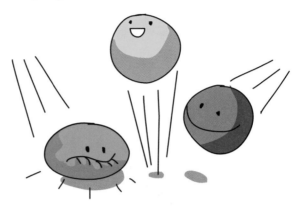

2. Paint the Dot

Click the **Paint new sprite** button (which looks like a paintbrush) next to New sprite.

   A new sprite named Sprite1 is created in the Sprite List. Clicking this button also switches to the Costumes tab, which contains the Paint Editor. Use the Brush tool to draw a small red dot near the crosshairs in the Paint Editor. It might help to zoom in by clicking the Zoom button (which looks like a magnifying glass) in the Paint Editor.

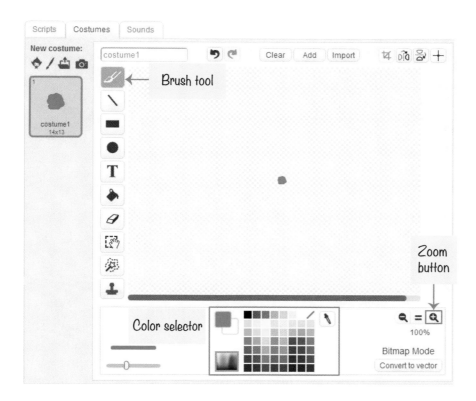

Click the ⓘ button for the `Sprite1` dot sprite to open its Info Area. (You can also open the Info Area by right-clicking the sprite and selecting **info**.)

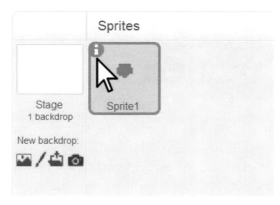

Change the sprite's name from Sprite1 to Dot 1. Then click the ◀ button to close the Info Area and display the Sprite List again.

3. Add Code for the Dot 1 Sprite

Now we can start programming. Click the **Scripts** tab to make the Scripts Area visible. Add the following code to the Scripts Area. You can find these blocks in the *Events* (brown), *Motion* (dark blue), *Operators* (green), and *Control* (yellow) categories. If you have trouble understanding how to drag these blocks, view the animation at *https://www.nostarch.com/scratchplayground/*.

```
when [flag] clicked
point in direction (pick random (-180) to (180))
forever
    move (10) steps
    if on edge, bounce
```

When you click the green flag, the Dot 1 sprite points in a random direction between −180 and 180 degrees. Then, the **forever** loop moves the sprite forward 10 steps and makes the sprite bounce when it hits the edge of the Stage. The sprite will continue to do this forever.

Notice that the Dot 1 sprite isn't drawing any rainbow lines yet. We'll do that later when we've created more sprites.

EXPLORE: DIRECTION AND DEGREES

Words like *up* or *right* are perfectly understood as directions by humans like you and me. But the computer needs a number to indicate an exact direction. All sprites in Scratch have their own direction number. The direction numbers are between −180 and 180 degrees. Pointing at 0 degrees is facing up. Pointing at 90 degrees is facing to the right. The following figure shows several directions and their degrees. Notice that the degrees increase in the clockwise direction and decrease in the counterclockwise direction. Also, notice that −180 and 180 degrees point in the same direction: down.

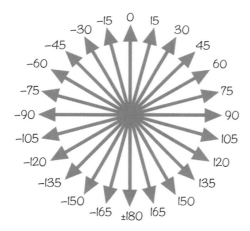

The **pick random -180 to 180** block chooses a random number to use as the direction. Then the **point in direction** block points the sprite in that direction. This means that the sprite could be pointed in any possible direction.

Let's write a new script that demonstrates how degrees work. Open a new tab by pressing CTRL-T in your web browser, and go to *https://scratch.mit.edu/* to open a new Scratch editor. You can edit multiple Scratch programs at the same time.

(continued)

In the Scripts Area for the cat sprite named Sprite1, add the following code using blocks from the *Events* (brown), *Control* (yellow), *Motion* (dark blue), and *Looks* (purple) categories. Keep in mind that we're writing a totally separate program from the *Rainbow Lines* program!

When you run this program, the cat sprite points toward the mouse. The cat will say the direction in which it's pointing.

Notice that the direction number changes as the cat's direction changes.

4. Duplicate the Dot 1 Sprite

Right-click the Dot 1 sprite in the Sprite List and select **duplicate**. Do this twice so that you make two duplicates: Dot 2 and Dot 3. (Scratch automatically names the sprites with increasing numbers.)

SAVE POINT

Click the green flag to test the code so far. Check that all three dots are moving and bouncing around the Stage. When you duplicated the sprites, you also duplicated the sprite code. Click the red stop sign and save your program.

C DRAW THE RAINBOW LINES

Now that we've created all the bouncing dots, we can create a fourth dot sprite to draw the rainbow lines. We'll write a program that makes this drawing dot move quickly between the three bouncing dot sprites, drawing a line as it moves. This process will repeat three times, and then after 10 seconds the screen will clear.

5. Add the Code for the Drawing Dot Sprite

Right-click one of the bouncing dot sprites and select **duplicate**. Because this is a duplicate of the bouncing dots, it has some code we need to delete. In its Scripts Area, delete all the code blocks by right-clicking the **when green flag clicked** block and then selecting **delete**. You can also delete blocks by dragging them to the Blocks Area in the middle of the editor, where they'll disappear.

Click the ⓘ button and rename this sprite Drawing Dot.

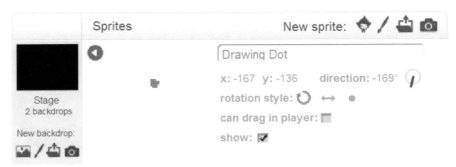

Add the following two scripts to the Drawing Dot sprite. You can find these blocks in the *Events* (brown), *Pen* (turquoise), *Control* (yellow), and *Motion* (dark blue) categories.

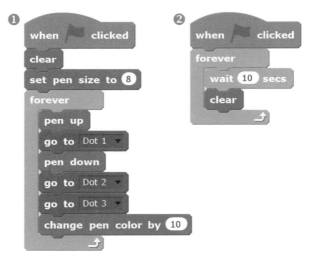

In script ❶, make sure you use the **go to** block, not the **go to x y** block. Also, be sure to change the **go to** blocks so they aren't going to the mouse-pointer. To do so, click the black triangle on the block and select a sprite from the menu.

Before you run the code, let's talk through how it works. When you click the green flag in script ❶, the Drawing Dot sprite runs the **clear** block to clear away any pen drawing already on the Stage. Then the script runs the **pen down** block: as the sprite moves around, it draws a line on the Stage.

To better understand what the **pen down** block does, imagine holding down a marker on a piece of paper while you walk around it: a line would be drawn following you! The drawing dot goes to Dot 1, puts its pen down, goes to Dot 2, and then goes to Dot 3. Next, the **change pen color by 10** block changes the color of the pen slightly. (You can increase this number to make the colors change faster.) At the same time, Dot 1, Dot 2, and Dot 3 sprites continue to move around on their own. So the V line that the Drawing Dot sprite draws also moves around.

Script ❷ is a lot simpler to understand. This code waits 10 seconds and then clears the screen of any marks made by the *Pen* blocks. Now the Stage won't become overcrowded with rainbow lines.

SAVE POINT

Click the green flag to test the code so far. You should see a flying rainbow V move across the Stage. Then, every 10 seconds, the rainbows clear. Click the red stop sign and save your program!

THE COMPLETE PROGRAM

The final code for the entire program is shown here. Notice that the code for Dot 1, Dot 2, and Dot 3 sprites is identical. If your program isn't working correctly, check your code against this code:

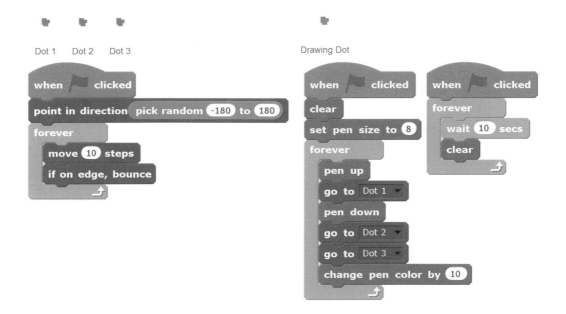

Dot 1   Dot 2   Dot 3

```
when [flag] clicked
point in direction  pick random -180 to 180
forever
    move 10 steps
    if on edge, bounce
```

Drawing Dot

```
when [flag] clicked
clear
set pen size to 8
forever
    pen up
    go to  Dot 1 ▼
    pen down
    go to  Dot 2 ▼
    go to  Dot 3 ▼
    change pen color by 10
```

```
when [flag] clicked
forever
    wait 10 secs
    clear
```

TURBO MODE

If you hold SHIFT while click-ing the green flag, you can start the program in Turbo Mode. The computer is usually able to run code blocks quickly, but a program that draws sprites to the screen slows down the computer. In Turbo Mode, instead of drawing the screen after each code block, Scratch only draws to the screen after several code blocks. Human eyes won't notice the skipped drawings, and the program will look like it's running faster.

SHIFT-click the green flag to run the *Rainbow Lines* program in Turbo Mode. Almost instantly, the screen fills up! To end Turbo Mode, SHIFT-click the green flag again.

VERSION 2.0: RAINBOW TRIANGLES

Your *Rainbow Lines* program is complete as it is, but you can take this program to the next level. You can always think of new ideas to add to your programs after you have the basics working.

For version 2.0 of the program, let's connect Dot 3 and Dot 1 so that, instead of a flying rainbow *V*, the program has a flying rainbow triangle. Modify the code for the Drawing Dot sprite to match the following, but leave the rest of the code the same.

```
when 🏳 clicked
clear
set pen size to 8
forever
    pen up
    go to Dot 1 ▼
    pen down
    go to Dot 2 ▼
    go to Dot 3 ▼
    go to Dot 1 ▼
    change pen color by 10
```

The new **go to Dot 1** block draws a line from Dot 3 to
Dot 1, forming a triangle.

SAVE POINT

Click the green flag to test the code so far. Make sure you see
a flying rainbow triangle moving around the Stage. Then click
the red stop sign and save your program.

VERSION 3.0:
TWO RAINBOW LINES

For version 3.0, let's create two separate flying lines instead of
a single line.

Right-click the Dot 3 sprite and select **duplicate** to make
a Dot 4 sprite. Then modify the Drawing Dot sprite's code to
match the following.

```
when [flag] clicked
clear
set pen size to (8)
forever
    pen up
    go to [Dot 1 ▼]
    pen down
    go to [Dot 2 ▼]
    pen up
    go to [Dot 3 ▼]
    pen down
    go to [Dot 4 ▼]
    change pen color by (10)
```

The new code puts the pen down while moving between Dot 1 and Dot 2. Then it lifts the pen up, goes to Dot 3, and puts the pen down again to draw a line from Dot 3 to Dot 4.

SAVE POINT

Click the green flag to test the code so far. Make sure you see two flying rainbow lines. Then click the red stop sign and save your program.

VERSION 4.0: YOU DECIDE!

You can start making your own changes to create new demoscene programs. In this chapter's program you drew lines, but if you learn the mathematics behind Bézier curves, you can make beautiful curves. Another mathematical concept that produces beautiful images is fractals, as shown in the following figure. Go to the Scratch website and search for "bézier," "fractals," or "demoscene" to get ideas for your own programs. You can also look at the code blocks for every Scratch program by clicking the **See inside** button on the program's web page. Check out some example projects at *https://www.nostarch.com/scratchplayground/*.

SUMMARY

In this chapter, you built a project that

▶ Has custom sprites that you created (even if they are just dots)

▶ Uses the **pick random** block to point a sprite in a random direction

▶ Makes sprites move and bounce off the edges of the Stage

▶ Duplicates sprites and their code

▶ Uses the *Pen* blocks to draw rainbow lines

This project is a demo that users can watch but can't control. In Chapter 3, you'll make a maze game that lets players interact with the program by using the keyboard instead of just watching. This will be the first real game project in this book!

REVIEW QUESTIONS

Try to answer the following practice questions to test what you've learned. You probably won't know all the answers off the top of your head, but you can explore the Scratch editor to figure out the answers. (The answers are also online at *http://www.nostarch.com/scratchplayground/*.)

1. What happens when a sprite moves after it has run the pen down block?

2. Some code moves a sprite, but no line is drawn behind it. What might cause this bug?

3. Which block causes the lines in the *Rainbow Lines* program to look like a rainbow?

4. Which code block do you use to make the rainbow lines thicker?

5. How do you turn on Turbo Mode? How do you turn it off?

6. How do you duplicate a sprite and its code blocks?

7. Where does a sprite point when its direction is 90 degrees?

8. What is the degree direction for pointing up?

9. You want a sprite to point down and move in that direction. In which color of blocks category would you find code blocks to do this?

10. How do you select a new backdrop from Scratch's Backdrop Library?

11. You see a sprite named Sprite1 in the Sprite List. How do you rename this sprite?

3
MAZE RUNNER

ou've probably played a maze game before, but have you ever tried making one? Mazes can be tricky to complete, but they're easy to program. In this chapter, you'll create a game that lets the player guide a cat through a maze to reach its goal—a delicious apple! You'll learn how to move the cat with the keyboard and how to block its progress with walls.

Before you start coding, take a look at the final program. Go to *https://www.nostarch.com/scratchplayground/* and play the game.

Your goal is to get the apple!

You control the cat.

SKETCH OUT THE DESIGN

First, draw what you want the game to look like on paper. With some planning, you can make your maze game a-maze-ing. (I never apologize for my puns.) My sketch for the maze game looks like the following figure.

Keep the cat from walking through walls.

Make a goal at the end of the maze.

Make the maze levels.

Make the cat walk around.

If you want to save time, you can start from the skeleton project file, named *maze-skeleton.sb2*, in the resources ZIP file. Go to *https://www.nostarch.com/scratchplayground/* and download the ZIP file to your computer by right-clicking the link and selecting **Save link as** or **Save target as**. Extract all the files from the ZIP file. The skeleton project file has all the sprites already loaded, so you'll only need to drag the code blocks into each sprite. Click **File ▶ Upload from your computer** in the Scratch editor to load the *maze-skeleton .sb2* file.

Even if you don't use the skeleton project, you should download the ZIP file from the website. This file contains the maze images you'll use in this chapter.

If you want to create everything on your own, click File ▶ New to start a new Scratch project. In the text field in the upper left, rename the project from *Untitled* to *Maze Runner*.

A MAKE THE CAT WALK AROUND

In the *Maze Runner* game, the player will control the cat sprite. In Part A, you'll set up the code to control the cat with the arrow keys on the keyboard.

EXPLORE: X- AND Y-COORDINATES

To make the cat move around the Stage, you need to use coordinates. *Coordinates* are numbers that represent an exact location. The x-coordinate (also called *x position*) is a number that represents how far left or right a sprite is on the Stage. In other words, **x** is the sprite's *horizontal* position. The y-coordinate (also called *y position*) is a number that represents how far up or down a sprite is on the Stage. The y-coordinate is a sprite's *vertical* position.

Used together, x- and y-coordinates indicate a sprite's precise location on the Stage. When writing coordinates, the x-coordinate always comes first, and the coordinates are separated by a comma. For example, an x-coordinate of 42 and a y-coordinate of 100 would look like this: (42, 100).

In the very center of the Stage is a point marked (0, 0), which is called the *origin*. In the following figure, I'm using the xy-grid backdrop from the Scratch Backdrop Library. (To load the xy-grid backdrop, click the **Choose backdrop from library** button next to the New backdrop label and select the backdrop.) I've added several cat sprites who are all saying their x- and y-coordinates.

The rightmost side of the Stage has an x-coordinate of 240. The x-coordinates get smaller as you go left. In the center, the x-coordinate is 0. To the left of the center, the x-coordinates become negative numbers. The leftmost side of the Stage has an x-coordinate of −240. The y-coordinates work the same way: the top of the Stage has a y-coordinate of 180, the center is 0, and the bottom is −180.

The mouse cursor's x- and y-coordinates are also given in the bottom-right corner of the Stage. In the previous figure, the mouse cursor is at the coordinates (−182, −27), which means the x-coordinate is −182 and the y-coordinate is −27.

Scratch displays the x- and y-coordinates of the currently selected sprite in the upper-right corner of the Scripts Area. Sprites move around the Stage when you change their x- and y-coordinates as shown here:

To make a sprite go . . .	change its . . .	by a . . .
Right	x-coordinate	positive number
Left	x-coordinate	negative number
Up	y-coordinate	positive number
Down	y-coordinate	negative number

(continued)

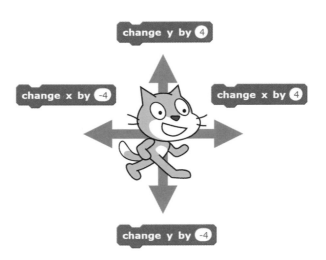

Many of the blocks in the dark blue *Motion* category will change a sprite's x and y position, such as the **change x by** and **change y by** blocks. Note that changing a coordinate by a negative number is the same as subtracting a positive number from it.

1. Add Movement Code to the Player Sprite

The first bit of code you'll add will make the arrow keys move the cat sprite, which is named Sprite1. But first, click ⓘ and rename this sprite Orange Cat. Then add the following code. You'll find these blocks in the *Events*, *Control*, *Sensing*, and *Motion* categories.

This code repeatedly checks whether the key is being pressed. The code literally reads "for forever, check whether the up arrow key is pressed, and if it is, then change **y** by 4."

If the up arrow key is not being pressed, Scratch skips the code inside the **if then** block.

Pressing the up arrow key makes the cat sprite move up. The **forever** loop block means Scratch will check over and over again whether the up arrow key is being pressed. This continues until you click the red stop sign.

The **forever** block is needed for this program to work. Without it, Scratch would only check *once* if the up arrow key was pressed. Then the program would end. But you want Scratch to keep checking forever if the up arrow key is pressed. If your program doesn't seem to be doing anything, make sure you didn't forget to add the **forever** block.

When you code this on your own, be sure you use the **change y by** code block instead of the **change x by** or **set y to** code blocks. If your program isn't working correctly, check that your code is the same as the code in this book.

SAVE POINT

Click the green flag and try moving the cat by pressing the up arrow key. Then click the red stop sign and save your program.

2. Duplicate the Movement Code for the Cat Sprite

Now you'll add code for the other three arrow keys: down, left, and right. This code is similar to the code to move the cat sprite up. To save time, you can right-click on the yellow **if then** block and select **duplicate** to create a copy of the blocks. These blocks will be identical, so all you'll need to change are the dark blue *Motion* blocks for the other directions. Duplicating blocks can often be faster than dragging new ones from the Blocks Area.

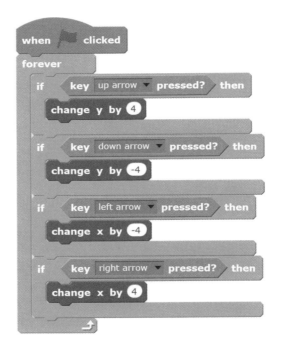

Scratch will now check if the four arrow keys are held down, one after another. After checking the right arrow key, Scratch starts back at the top of the loop and checks the up arrow key again. The computer checks them so fast that to human eyes it looks like all of the arrow keys are being checked at the same time!

SAVE POINT

Click the green flag to test the code so far. The cat should walk up, down, left, and right when you press the arrow keys. Notice that Orange Cat is small enough to fit in the maze you'll create next. Click the red stop sign and save your program.

If your program doesn't work and you don't know how to fix it, you can start over by using the *maze-part-a.sb2* Scratch project file, which is in the resources ZIP file. Click **File ▶ Upload from your computer** in the Scratch editor to load the *maze-part-a.sb2* file, and then move on to Part B.

B MAKE THE MAZE LEVELS

Next, we'll create the maze sprite and set the backdrop. The maze game would quickly get boring if it had only one maze, so we'll also add multiple levels to the game.

3. Download the Maze Images

You could draw the maze sprite yourself, but let's use images from the ZIP file instead. One of the maze images is the *Maze .sprite2* file.

In the Scratch editor, click the **Upload sprite from file** button and select *Maze.sprite2* to upload the file. This creates a new sprite named Maze with several maze costumes. Every sprite in Scratch can have multiple costumes to change the way it looks. These costumes, which you can see by clicking the **Costumes** tab, are often used to animate the sprite.

Your Sprite List should look like this:

4. Change the Backdrop

Let's add a little flair to the maze by placing some artwork in the background. You can use whichever background you like. Change the Stage's backdrop by clicking the **Choose backdrop from library** button under New backdrop to open the Scratch Backdrop Library window. Choose a background (I chose light), and click **OK**.

5. Start at the First Maze

Add the following code to the Maze sprite. You can find these blocks in the *Events*, *Looks*, and *Motion* categories.

Each of the Maze sprite's costumes will be a new level. When the player clicks the green flag to start the program, the game should begin with the first costume and make sure the maze is in the center of the Stage. We will add code to switch to the next level in Steps 8 and 9.

Note that the Scripts Area shows code blocks for the selected sprite. Be sure the Maze sprite is selected in the Sprite List; otherwise, you'll add the maze's code to a different sprite. Each sprite needs its own code to work correctly. If you don't see maze1 in the **switch costume to** block, the Orange Cat sprite is most likely selected.

If your Scratch program doesn't work and you don't know how to fix it, you can start over by using the *maze-part-b.sb2* Scratch project file, which is in the resources ZIP file. Click **File ▶ Upload from your computer** in the Scratch editor to load the *maze-part-b.sb2* file, and then move on to Part C.

ⓒ KEEP THE CAT FROM WALKING THROUGH WALLS

When you click the green flag now, you'll be able to move the cat through the maze. But you'll also be able to move the cat through the walls of the maze, because nothing in the program prevents this from happening. The code only states, "when the right arrow key is pressed, move the cat right." The cat moves, whether or not a wall is there.

6. Check Whether the Cat Is Touching the Walls

Let's add code that checks whether the cat is touching the blue walls. If it is, the cat should move backward. So if the cat moves to the right and is touching a wall, it should automatically move left. This will undo the player's move and prevent the cat from moving through walls. Click the Orange Cat sprite in the Sprite List, and modify the code to look like the following. Notice that we're using the **touching?** block, not the **touching color?** block.

Also, you might have noticed that the Orange Cat sprite is Godzilla-sized compared to the maze, making the cat look unrealistic. Add a **set size** block from the *Looks* category to make the Orange Cat sprite smaller. You also want the Orange Cat sprite to always be shown on top of the maze, so you'll add the **go to front** block. These two code blocks are at the top of the script.

SAVE POINT

Click the green flag to test the code so far. Make sure the Orange Cat sprite cannot walk through the maze walls. Test this for all four directions. Then click the red stop sign and save your program.

If your Scratch program doesn't work and you don't know how to fix it, you can start over by using the *maze-part-c.sb2* Scratch project file, which is in the resources ZIP file. Click **File ▶ Upload from your computer** in the Scratch editor to load the *maze-part-c.sb2* file, and then move on to Part D.

D MAKE A GOAL AT THE END OF THE MAZE

Right now, it isn't clear where the player is supposed to end up in the maze. Let's add an apple at the other end of the maze to make the player's goal more obvious.

7. Create the Apple Sprite

Click the **Choose sprite from library** button (which looks like a face) next to New sprite. When the Sprite Library window appears, select **Apple** and click **OK** to add a new sprite named Apple to the Sprite List.

When the game starts, you want the Apple sprite to move to the end of the maze at the top of the Stage. The Apple sprite also has to be small enough to fit in the maze. Add the following code to the Apple sprite:

8. Detect When the Player Reaches the Apple

The *Maze Runner* game has a sprite for the player, the maze, and the apple at the end of the maze. Now it just needs the code to detect when the player reaches the end. When that happens, you'll have Scratch play a sound and then swap costumes to the next level. But before you add the code, you need to load the cheer sound. Select Orange Cat in the Sprite List. Click the **Sounds** tab at the top of the Blocks Area, and then click the **Choose sound from library** button. This button looks like a speaker and is under New sound.

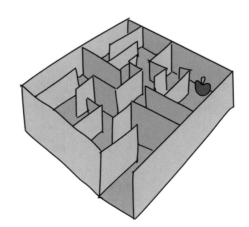

In the Sound Library window that appears, select cheer and then click **OK** to load the cheer sound. Now click the **Scripts** tab.

Add this script to the Orange Cat sprite's code:

To make the **broadcast** block broadcast the next maze message, click the black triangle in the **broadcast** block and select **new message**.

In the window that appears, type *next maze* as the message name and click **OK**.

9. Add the Broadcast Handling Code to the Maze Sprite

Click the Maze sprite in the Sprite List, and add the following code to it:

This code changes the maze level when it receives the next maze broadcast.

SAVE POINT

Click the green flag to test the code so far. Try playing the completed game. Make sure the level changes to the next maze when the cat touches the apple. Then click the red stop sign and save your program.

THE COMPLETE PROGRAM

The following code shows the entire program. If your program isn't working right, check your code against this complete code. The complete program is also in the resources ZIP file as the *maze .sb2* file.

I hope the code for this maze program isn't too labyrinthine.

Orange Cat

```
when [flag] clicked
go to front
set size to 15 %
go to x: 10 y: -170
forever
    if < key up arrow pressed? > then
        change y by 4
        if < touching Maze ? > then
            change y by -4

    if < key down arrow pressed? > then
        change y by -4
        if < touching Maze ? > then
            change y by 4

    if < key left arrow pressed? > then
        change x by -4
        if < touching Maze ? > then
            change x by 4

    if < key right arrow pressed? > then
        change x by 4
        if < touching Maze ? > then
            change x by -4
```

```
when [flag] clicked
forever
    if < touching Apple ? > then
        play sound cheer
        say Yay! for 2 secs
        go to x: 10 y: -170
        broadcast next maze
```

Maze

```
when [flag] clicked
switch costume to maze1
go to x: 0 y: 0
```

```
when I receive next maze
next costume
```

Apple

```
when [flag] clicked
set size to 25 %
go to x: -10 y: 170
```

VERSION 2.0: TWO-PLAYER MODE

Now that the basic maze game is working, you can do some iterative development and add small improvements one at a time. Iterative development helps you avoid trying to make a game that is too large for you to finish.

In version 2.0 of *Maze Runner*, you'll add a second player. The two players will race against one another. The first player starts at the bottom and races to the top; the second player races from the top to the bottom. Because they both must travel the same path, the distance for each is the same.

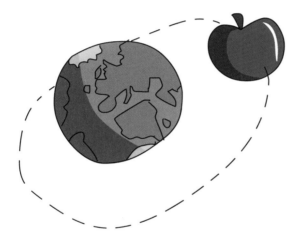

Duplicate the Apple Sprite

The second player needs a goal too. Right-click the Apple sprite and select **duplicate** to make a copy of the Apple sprite and its code. The new sprite is automatically named Apple2. Select the Apple2 sprite, and click the **Costumes** tab. Select a green color from the bottom, and then select the **Fill** tool to the right (it looks like a tipped cup). Then click the red part of the apple to change it to green. When you're done, Apple2 will look like the following figure.

3 Click the center of the apple.

1 Select the green color.

2 Click the Fill tool.

Modify the Apple2 Sprite's Code

You need to modify the Apple2 sprite's code to look like the following code so that the green apple starts at the bottom of the maze rather than the top:

Duplicate the Orange Cat Sprite

Now let's add a second cat sprite. Right-click the Orange Cat sprite and select **duplicate** from the menu to make a copy of Orange Cat and its code. The new sprite is automatically named Orange Cat2. The Orange Cat and Orange Cat2 sprites need to look different enough that the players can tell them apart. Similar to what you did for Apple2, click the **Costumes** tab and change Orange Cat2 from orange to blue.

Click on the ⓘ button and rename Orange Cat2 to Blue Cat.

Modify the Code for the Blue Cat Sprite

Right now the Blue Cat sprite has the same code as the Orange Cat sprite. You'll need to change the code; otherwise, the arrow keys will control both player 1 and player 2. The second player will control the Blue Cat sprite using the WASD keys (pronounced *whaz-dee*). The W, A, S, and D keys are often used as a left-handed version of the up, left, down, and right arrow keys.

Change the two **go to x y** blocks and the **key pressed?** blocks for Blue Cat to look like the following code. Also, remember to change **if touching Apple** to **if touching Apple2**.

```
when [flag] clicked
go to front
set size to (15) %
go to x: (-10) y: (170)        ◄—————————— Changed x and y
forever
    if < key (w ▼) pressed? > then    ◄—————————— Changed the key
        change y by (4)
        if < touching (Maze ▼) ? > then
            change y by (-4)

    if < key (s ▼) pressed? > then    ◄—————————— Changed the key
        change y by (-4)
        if < touching (Maze ▼) ? > then
            change y by (4)

    if < key (a ▼) pressed? > then    ◄—————————— Changed the key
        change x by (-4)
        if < touching (Maze ▼) ? > then
            change x by (4)

    if < key (d ▼) pressed? > then    ◄—————————— Changed the key
        change x by (4)
        if < touching (Maze ▼) ? > then
            change x by (-4)
```

```
when [flag] clicked
forever
    if < touching (Apple ▼) ? > then    ◄—————————— Changed sprite
        play sound (cheer ▼)
        say (Yay!) for (2) secs
        go to x: (10) y: (-170)          ◄—————————— Changed x and y
        broadcast (next maze ▼)
```

Go Back to the Starting Position

The sprites go back to their starting positions when they touch their apples, but they also need to go there when the other cat wins. Add the following script to the **Orange Cat** sprite:

And then add the following script to the **Blue Cat** sprite:

This way, when the other cat wins and broadcasts the next maze message, both cats will go back to their starting positions.

SAVE POINT

Click the green flag to test the code so far. Try moving both players using the arrow keys and the WASD keys. Make sure each of the eight keys moves the correct cat and only that cat. Try playing the full game. Make sure the level changes to the next maze when the second player touches the green apple. Make sure both players are sent to their starting points when the next level begins. Click the red stop sign and save your program.

You've just upgraded your maze game to support two players. Find a friend to race against! Player 1 uses the arrow keys, and player 2 uses the WASD keys.

VERSION 3.0: TRAPS

After you've played *Maze Runner* against another player a few times, running through the mazes can become too easy. Let's make *Maze Runner* a bit more difficult by adding spike traps. The spike traps will shoot out spikes and then retract them. If a player touches the trap while the spikes are out, the player will slow down. This gives the other player time to race ahead!

Draw a New Sprite for the Traps

Click the **Paint new sprite** button next to New sprite to draw a new sprite. This sprite will have two different costumes that we draw: one costume with the spikes retracted and another with the spikes out. But don't worry, the spike trap drawings are simple. Just click the **Line** tool and the color black to draw a simple line, which is what the spike trap looks like when the spikes are retracted. Rename this costume trap off.

Create a Second Costume for the Traps

The spike trap sprite needs a second costume to show what it looks like when the spikes are out. Right-click trap off (the single line you drew) and select **duplicate** to create trap off2. In trap off2, select a gray color and draw the spikes coming out of the single line. Rename this costume trap on.

Make sure the spike trap is small enough to fit in the maze. To shrink it, click the **Shrink** tool (as shown in the following figure), and then click the sprite on the Stage. Click the **Shrink** tool as many times as necessary to shrink it to the right size.

Also, click the ⓘ button for the sprite to open its Info Area, and rename it Trap.

Add Cloning Code for the Traps

Because you'll want several traps in the maze, you could duplicate the Trap sprite, but there's a better way. You can use the clone blocks to make clones of the Trap sprite. Make the Trap sprite's code look like this:

```
when 🚩 clicked
show
repeat 6
    create clone of myself ▼
hide
```

```
when I start as a clone
go to x: pick random -170 to 170 y: pick random -170 to 170
wait 2 secs
forever
    switch costume to trap off ▼
    wait pick random 5 to 8 secs
    switch costume to trap on ▼
    wait pick random 1 to 4 secs
```

The **repeat 6** loop will run the **create clone of myself** block six times to make six clones. These clones will then run the code in the **when I start as a clone** block. This script first moves the Trap sprites to random positions in the maze. After the **wait 2 secs** block pauses them for a bit, the **forever** loop switches between the trap off and trap on costumes, which sticks out and retracts the spikes.

SAVE POINT

Click the green flag to test the code so far. Try moving both players using the arrow keys and the WASD keys. Make sure each of the eight keys moves the correct cat and only that cat. Try playing the full game. Make sure the level changes to the next maze when the second player touches the green apple. Make sure both players are sent to their starting points when the next level begins. Click the red stop sign and save your program.

Modify the Orange Cat Code

Right now, the cats aren't programmed to do anything when they touch the spikes. Select Orange Cat in the Sprite List, and add the following code to the *bottom* of the existing code inside the **forever** block. To set the color in the **touching color?** block, click the color square in the block. The next color you click in the Scratch editor will become the selected color. Click the Trap sprite spikes in the Sprite List to set the **touching color?** block to gray. (If you don't see the spikes, click the Trap sprite in the Sprite List, click the **Costumes** tab, and then select trap on. The costume with the spikes appears for the sprite in the Sprite List.) Add the following code to the script with the **key pressed?** blocks:

The cat can walk over the trap clones just fine when the spikes are retracted, because the gray color is not shown. But if the spikes are out, the cat will touch the gray color and pause to say "Ouch!" for 2 seconds.

SAVE POINT

Click the green flag to test the code so far. Try moving the orange cat over the traps when the spikes are in and out. The cat should only say "Ouch!" when the spikes are out. Click the red stop sign and save your program.

Copy the Code from Orange Cat to Blue Cat

The second player's cat, Blue Cat, also needs the code for setting the color in the **touching color?** block. You can use this shortcut: click and drag the yellow part of the **if touching color? then** block in Orange Cat and drop it over Blue Cat in the Sprite List. The code block will move back to its original place in Orange Cat and will also be duplicated in Blue Cat. This duplicating technique is usually faster than dragging new blocks from the Blocks Area.

Select Blue Cat in the Sprite List. Move the duplicated code to the bottom of the **forever** loop. The code looks the same as the code in Orange Cat. The following figure shows how to drag and duplicate these code blocks.

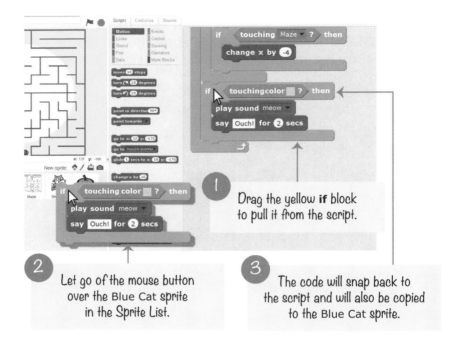

1 Drag the yellow **if** block to pull it from the script.

2 Let go of the mouse button over the Blue Cat sprite in the Sprite List.

3 The code will snap back to the script and will also be copied to the Blue Cat sprite.

You've finished version 3.0 of *Maze Runner*. With traps and two players, *Maze Runner* is now more interesting than the basic 1.0 version. You can always come up with new features you want to add on your own. But first, let's add some secret cheats that players can use to hack the game.

CHEAT MODE: WALK THROUGH WALLS

Teleporting is a cool cheat, but players can't control where they teleport to. Also, it's too obvious that a player is cheating when they suddenly move across the Stage and through many walls. However, you can add a more subtle cheat that lets the cats move through walls when a special key is held down.

Add the Walk-Through-Walls Code to Orange Cat

For the Orange Cat sprite, modify the walking code so the **touching Maze?** blocks are replaced with the **touching Maze? and not key l pressed?** blocks. Only the code for the up arrow is shown here, but you'll want to replace the **touching Maze?** blocks in all four of the **if key pressed** cases.

This enables the wall-blocking code only if the L key is *not* being pressed. If the L key *is* pressed, this wall-blocking code is skipped, and the player walks through the walls.

Add the Walk-Through-Walls Code to Blue Cat

Make the same walk-through-walls code changes to the Blue Cat sprite, except instead of **key l pressed**, make it **key q pressed**. The second player can walk through walls when the Q key is held down.

SAVE POINT

Click the green flag to test the code so far. Try walking through the walls by holding down the L or Q key. Make sure both cats can walk through walls but only when holding down the correct key. Click the red stop sign and save your program.

 With this cheat code in the program, you can hack the game and make your cat walk through walls. The wall cheat shows you that anything is possible in your Scratch programs!

SUMMARY

In this chapter, you built a game that

▶ Has a cat sprite that can walk up, down, left, and right when the player presses certain keys

▶ Has walls that the sprites can't walk through

▶ Broadcasts messages from one sprite that another sprite can receive

▶ Has a maze sprite with eight different costumes

▶ Supports two players using different keyboard keys

▶ Adds traps that turn on at random intervals to delay players

▶ Includes cheat modes that let the cats walk through walls

A two-player game is more exciting than a single-player game. Now, instead of just solving a maze, you are racing against another player! And you get to show off your Scratch game to someone else.

In Chapter 4, you'll work with a basketball game. This game uses a side view, unlike the maze's bird's-eye view. But this means you'll be able to add jumping and gravity, which are great techniques to use in many types of Scratch games!

REVIEW QUESTIONS

Try to answer the following practice questions to test what you've learned. You probably won't know all the answers off the top of your head, but you can explore the Scratch editor to figure out the answers. (The answers are also online at *http://www.nostarch.com/scratchplayground/*.)

1. Which block will change the size of a sprite?
2. How can the code in one sprite send a message to another sprite to do something?
3. How might you use the WASD keys on the keyboard?
4. How can you duplicate some code blocks from one sprite to another sprite?
5. What will happen if you accidentally use a **change y** by code block instead of a **change x** by code block?
6. If you want a sprite to play the cheer sound, how do you load this sound?
7. Look at the following code. It lets the player press the arrow keys to move the sprite left and right. It works, but what would you change to make the sprite walk faster?

4

SHOOTING HOOPS
WITH GRAVITY

any platformer games, such as *Super Mario Bros.* and *Donkey Kong Country*, show a side view of the action, where the bottom of the screen is the ground and the character is shown from the side. These games have *gravity*: characters can jump up and then fall until they land on the ground. In this chapter, we'll write a basketball game that has gravity. The player will jump and throw a basketball, and the basketball player and ball will fall downward.

Before you start coding, look at the final program at
https://www.nostarch.com/scratchplayground/.

SKETCH OUT THE DESIGN

First, let's sketch out what we want the game to do. The player
controls the cat, which can move left and right and jump. The
goal is to have the cat shoot baskets into a moving basketball
hoop, which will glide around the Stage randomly.

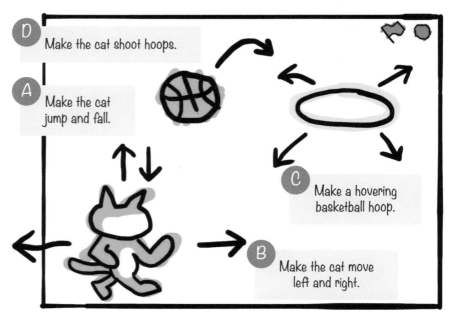

D Make the cat shoot hoops.

A Make the cat jump and fall.

C Make a hovering basketball hoop.

B Make the cat move left and right.

If you want to save time, you can start from the skeleton project file, named *basketball-skeleton.sb2*, in the resources ZIP file. Go to *https://www.nostarch.com/scratchplayground/* and download the ZIP file to your computer by right-clicking the link and selecting **Save link as** or **Save target as**. Extract all the files from the ZIP file. The skeleton project file has all the sprites already loaded, so you'll only need to drag the code blocks into each sprite.

Ⓐ MAKE THE CAT JUMP AND FALL

Let's start by adding gravity to make the cat jump up and fall down.

1. Add the Gravity Code to the Cat Sprite

Click the ❶ button for the Sprite1 sprite to open its Info Area. Rename the sprite Cat, and then close the Info Area. Then rename the program from *Untitled* to *Basketball* in the text field at the top of the Scratch editor.

Click the **Choose backdrop from library** button under New backdrop to open the Backdrop Library window. Select **brick wall1** and click **OK** to change the backdrop. The Stage will look like this:

Programming gravity requires *variables*. You can think of a variable as a box for storing numbers or text that you can use later in your program. We'll create a variable that contains a number representing how fast the cat is falling.

First, make sure the Cat sprite is selected in the Sprite List and then click the Scripts tab. In the orange *Data* category, click the **Make a Variable** button to bring up the New Variable window. Enter y velocity as the variable name. (*Velocity* means how fast something is going and in what direction. When y velocity is a positive number, the cat moves up. When y velocity is a negative number, the cat moves down.) Make sure **For this sprite only** is selected. (If you see only For all sprites, the Stage is selected, not the Cat sprite.) Then click **OK**.

Several new blocks will appear in the *Data* category, and one of those is the round y velocity variable block, shown here:

EXPLORE: FOR ALL SPRITES VS. FOR THIS SPRITE ONLY

When you create the y velocity variable, you have to select **For this sprite only**. This option creates a variable that *only* the Cat sprite can use. The For all sprites option will create a variable that all sprites can use.

To identify the kind of variable you've created, check the box next to the round variable block in the Blocks Area to make the variable appear on the Stage. If you selected For this sprite only, the sprite name will display in front of the variable name. But if you selected For all sprites, only the variable name will show.

The Cat sprite name before y velocity means that this is a For this sprite only variable.

Check this box to make the variable visible on the Stage.

If you made a mistake and the sprite name Cat does not appear at the start of the variable name in your program, right-click the **y velocity** block in the orange *Data* category and select **delete variable** from the menu. Then create the y velocity variable again, making sure you select **For this sprite only**.

As with any variable block, you can place the y velocity block anywhere you would normally enter a number or some text. The code block will use the number or text set in the variable. When you use variables, your program can change the variable's number or text *while the program is running*.

To put a value in your variable, you use the orange **set to** block. For example, if you created a variable greeting, you could use **set to** to put the value Hello! in it. Then, you could use greeting in a **say** block, which would be the same as entering Hello!. (Don't add these blocks or create a greeting variable in your *Basketball* program; this is just an example.)

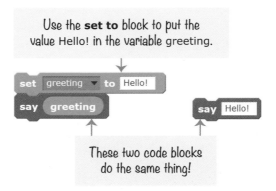

If you want to change the greeting text while the program is running, you can add another **set to** block to your program. If the variable contains a number, you can add to or subtract from this number by using the **change by** block.

Gravity makes objects *accelerate* downward. In the game, the Cat sprite has to move down, and the speed at which it moves down must change *while the program is running*. Add the following code to the Cat sprite to add gravity to your Scratch program. This is the minimal amount of code you need to make a sprite fall under gravity. You could add this code to any sprite to make it fall.

When you click the green flag, the y velocity variable is set to 0, and then the script enters a **forever** loop. The y position (vertical position) of the Cat sprite is changed by y velocity, and y velocity is changed by -2. As the program goes through the loop, the y position will change faster and faster, making the cat fall faster and faster.

SAVE POINT

Before you click the green flag, drag the Cat sprite to the top of the Stage. When you click the green flag, notice that the cat begins to fall. If you want the cat to fall again, click the red stop sign, move the Cat sprite back to the top of the Stage, and click the green flag again. Save your program.

2. Add the Ground Level Code

Right now, the cat falls. But we want the cat to stop when it hits the ground. Let's keep adding to the Cat sprite's code so it looks this:

In this code, we set the **y position** of the ground level to -130. If the Cat sprite's y position is greater than (above) the ground level, then y velocity is changed by -2 and the Cat sprite will fall. Eventually, the Cat sprite will fall past -130, and its y position will be less than (below) the -130 ground level. When that happens, the Cat sprite will be reset at the ground level of -130, and y velocity will go back to 0 to stop the sprite from falling.

SAVE POINT

Click the green flag to test the code so far. Drag the cat up using your mouse, and let go. Make sure the cat falls to the ground but does not fall past the edge of the Stage. You can experiment with different ground levels by changing -130 to another number. Then click the red stop sign and save your program.

When you're done testing your program, make the y velocity variable invisible on the Stage by unchecking the checkbox next to it in the orange *Data* category.

3. Add the Jumping Code to the Cat Sprite

After adding the gravity code to the Cat sprite, making the cat jump is easy. Add this code to the Cat sprite:

Now when you press the up arrow key, y velocity is set to the positive number 20, making the Cat sprite jump up. But the y velocity variable will still be changed by -2 each time the loop runs. So although the cat jumps by 20 at first, the next time through the loop it will be at 18, then 16, and so on. Notice that the **if then** block checks that the Cat sprite is on the ground. You shouldn't be able to make the cat jump if it's already in midair!

When y velocity is set to 0, the Cat sprite is at the peak of the jump. Then y velocity changes by -2 each time through the loop, and the Cat sprite continues falling until it hits the ground. Try experimenting with different numbers for the **set y velocity to** and **change y velocity by** blocks. Figure out how to make the cat jump higher or lower (but always above the ground) or make gravity stronger or weaker.

SAVE POINT

Click the green flag to test the code so far. Press the up arrow key, and make sure the cat jumps up and falls back down. Then click the red stop sign and save your program.

Ⓑ MAKE THE CAT MOVE LEFT AND RIGHT

Let's add the Cat sprite's walking code next so that the player can control the cat with the keyboard.

4. Add the Walking Code to the Cat Sprite

Add the following code to the bottom of the Cat sprite's code:

```
when [flag] clicked
forever
    if < key [left arrow ▼] pressed? > then
        next costume
        change x by (-10)
    if < key [right arrow ▼] pressed? > then
        next costume
        change x by (10)
```

Inside the **forever** loop, the program checks if the left arrow or right arrow key is being pressed. If it is, the Cat sprite switches to the next costume and changes its x position by -10 (moves to the left) or 10 (moves to the right). The Cat sprite comes with two costumes that you can view by clicking the Costumes tab above the Blocks Area. By switching between the two costumes using the **next costume** block, you can make it look like the cat is walking.

SAVE POINT

Click the green flag to test the code so far. Press the left and right arrow keys, and make sure the cat moves in the correct direction. It's okay if the cat walks backward when moving to the left; that's what we want. Then click the red stop sign and save your program.

MAKE A HOVERING BASKETBALL HOOP

Now that the Cat sprite is complete, let's move on to the next sprite in the game: the basketball hoop.

5. Create the Hoop Sprite

Click the **Paint new sprite** button next to New sprite. Before you start drawing, click the **Convert to vector** button in the lower-right corner. The drawing tool buttons will appear on the right side of the Paint Editor. (Vector mode lets you draw using shapes, rather than drawing the individual pixels of an image.) Click the yellow color and use the Ellipse tool to draw a hoop. You can also slide the Line width slider in the lower-left corner to make the ellipse's line thicker. Make sure the Paint Editor's crosshairs are in the center of the hoop.

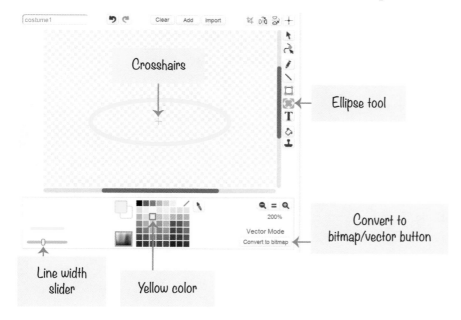

Rename the sprite Hoop in its Info Area. We want the Hoop sprite to play a cheer sound when the player makes a basket, so let's load the cheer sound next. Click the **Sounds** tab at the top of the Blocks Area, and then click the **Choose sound from library** button under New sound. When the Sound Library window opens, select cheer and click **OK**.

The cheer sound will now appear as an option for the **play sound** block you'll add to the Hoop sprite.

Add the following code to the Hoop sprite to make it glide randomly around the top half of the Stage. You'll need to create a broadcast message by clicking the **when I receive** block's black triangle and selecting **new message**. Name the new broadcast message swoosh.

Script ❶ makes the hoop slide to a new position every second. A moving hoop will make the game more challenging to play! Script ❷ plays the cheer sound and displays "Swoosh!" when the swoosh broadcast is received. Later, we'll make the Basketball sprite broadcast this message when a basket is made.

6. Create the Hitbox Sprite

Now let's think about how to create code that determines whether or not the player makes a basket. We could write a program that checks whether the basketball is simply *touching* the hoop. But because the hoop is so wide, just the edges of the basketball touching the hoop would count as a basket. We want the basket to count only if the basketball goes through the middle of the hoop. We'll have to think of a better fix.

If we simply checked whether the basketball was touching the hoop, this would count as a basket. But that's not how basketball works!

Instead, you can create a *hitbox*. A hitbox is a game-design term for a rectangular area that determines whether two game objects have collided with each other. We'll make a hitbox sprite. Create a new sprite by clicking the **Paint new sprite** button next to New sprite. Draw a small black square in the middle of the crosshairs by using the Rectangle tool and selecting the solid fill option. Rename this sprite Hitbox. The Hitbox sprite will look like this:

Rectangle tool

Solid fill

Add the following code to the Hitbox sprite:

The Hitbox sprite will now follow the Hoop sprite, no matter where it glides.

In Step 9, we'll write a program that makes sure a basket counts only if the basketball is touching the Hitbox sprite, not the Hoop sprite. The basketball will have to be much closer to the middle of the hoop to count as a basket!

It looks odd to see a black square in the middle of the Hoop sprite, so let's make the Hitbox sprite invisible. Add the **set ghost effect** block to the Hitbox sprite and set it to 100.

There's a difference between the **hide** block and the **set ghost effect to 100** block. If you used the **hide** block to make the Hitbox sprite invisible, the touching blocks would never detect that the ball was touching the Hitbox sprite, and the player would never be able to score. The **set ghost effect to 100** block makes the sprite invisible, but this block still allows the touching blocks to detect the Hitbox sprite's presence.

SAVE POINT

Click the green flag to test the code so far. Make sure the hoop glides around the Stage and the hitbox rectangle is always in the middle of it. Then click the red stop sign and save your program.

Ⓓ MAKE THE CAT SHOOT HOOPS

Next, you'll add a basketball for the cat to throw. Like the cat, the basketball will have gravity code and fall to the ground.

7. Create the Basketball Sprite

Click the **Choose sprite from library** button next to New sprite to open the Sprite Library window. Select the **Basketball** and click **OK**.

Next, click the **Sounds** tab at the top of the Blocks Area, and then click the **Choose sound from library** button next to New sound to open the Sound Library window. Select the pop sound and click **OK**. Click the **Scripts** tab at the top of the Blocks Area to bring back the Scripts Area.

Now go to the orange *Data* category. You'll make two variables. Click the **Make a Variable** button. Name the variable y velocity, and make sure **For this sprite only** is selected before you click **OK**. Because they are For this sprite only variables, the Basketball sprite's y velocity variable is separate from the Cat sprite's y velocity variable. Even though they have the same name, they are two different variables.

Click the **Make a Variable** button again to make another variable named Player 1 Score, but this time select **For all**

SHOOTING HOOPS WITH GRAVITY

sprites. (We capitalize Player 1 Score because we'll make it visible on the Stage. Uncheck the box next to y velocity to hide it on the Stage.) The new variable blocks should appear in the orange *Data* category.

8. Add the Code for the Basketball Sprite

After you've added the pop sound and two variables, add this code to the Basketball sprite:

Script ❶ makes sure the player starts with 0 points and hides the Basketball sprite to start.

Script ❷ uses code similar to the Cat sprite code. When the player presses the spacebar, the basketball appears in front of the cat and starts moving forward. The code sets the Basketball sprite's y velocity variable to a positive number, just like how the Cat sprite's y velocity variable is set to a positive number when the cat jumps; this is how the cat throws the ball.

The **repeat until y position < -130** block will keep the Basketball sprite falling until it reaches the ground. When it reaches the ground, the basketball will be hidden until the next time the player presses the spacebar.

SAVE POINT

Click the green flag to test the code so far. Press the spacebar to make the cat throw the basketball. Make sure the basketball disappears when it touches the ground. Then click the red stop sign and save your program.

9. Detect Whether a Basket Is Made

Next, you'll add the code that checks whether the Basketball sprite is touching the Hitbox sprite. This is how you know whether a basket has been made, and if it has, the Player 1 Score variable should increase. However, there is one snag: the basket shouldn't count if the basketball goes *up* through the hoop.

Keep in mind that if the y velocity variable is positive, the **change y by y velocity** block will move the Basketball sprite up. If y velocity is 0, then the Basketball sprite is not moving up or down. But if y velocity is a negative number, then the Basketball sprite will be falling down.

So you'll add another **if then** condition to the Basketball sprite's code. You'll increase the score only if the basketball is touching the hitbox (using the **touching Hitbox?** block) and falling *downward* (**y velocity < 0**).

```
when space ▼ key pressed
play sound pop ▼
go to Cat ▼
set y velocity ▼ to 24
show
repeat until < y position < -130 >
    change x by 8
    change y by y velocity
    change y velocity ▼ by -2
    turn ↻ 6 degrees
    if < touching Hitbox ▼ ? and < y velocity < 0 >> then
        change Player 1 Score ▼ by 1
        broadcast swoosh ▼
hide
```

The **and** block combines two conditions. For Scratch to run
the code blocks inside the **if then** block, *both* of these conditions
must be true. It isn't enough for the sprite to be touching the
Hitbox sprite *or* for the y velocity variable to be less than 0.
Both **touching Hitbox?** *and* **y velocity < 0** must be true for
the player to score. If these conditions are true, the Player 1
Score variable is increased by 1 and the swoosh message is
broadcasted.

SAVE POINT

Click the green flag to test the code so far. Shoot some baskets. The Player 1 Score variable should increase only if the
basketball touches the center of the hoop and is moving down.
The Hoop sprite should also say *swoosh* and play the cheer
sound when this happens. Click the red stop sign and save
your program.

10. Fix the Scoring Bug

Did you notice that Player 1 Score increases by several points for a single basket? This is a *bug*, which is a problem that makes the program behave in an unexpected way. We'll need to take another careful look at the code to figure out why this happens.

The **repeat until** loop block keeps looping until the ball hits the ground, so all of this code is for a single throw. The **repeat until** loop block checks several times whether or not the Basketball sprite is touching the Hitbox sprite and falling down. The Player 1 Score should increase only the first time.

You fix this bug by creating a new variable that keeps track of the first time the basketball touches the hoop for a single throw. Then you can make sure the player scores a point only once per throw.

Click the orange *Data* category at the top of the Blocks Area, and then click **Make a Variable**. Name the variable made basket and select **For this sprite only**. Then modify the Basketball sprite code.

```
when space ▼ key pressed
set made basket ▼ to no
play sound pop ▼
go to Cat ▼
set y velocity ▼ to 24
show
repeat until  y position < -130
    change x by 8
    change y by y velocity
    change y velocity ▼ by -2
    turn ↻ 6 degrees
    if  touching Hitbox ▼ ?  and  y velocity < 0  and  made basket = no  then
        change Player 1 Score ▼ by 1
        set made basket ▼ to yes
        broadcast swoosh ▼
hide
```

The made basket variable is set to no when the player first presses the spacebar. This makes sense because the player has not made a basket when the ball is initially thrown. We'll also use an **and** block to add another condition to the code that checks whether a basket has been made. A basket is now detected and the code in the **if then** block is run when three conditions are true:

1. The Basketball sprite is touching the Hitbox sprite.
2. The y velocity variable is negative (the basketball is falling down).
3. The made basket variable is set to no.

The first time the Basketball sprite detects it has made a basket, it increases Player 1 Score by 1 point and sets made basket to yes. In future checks for that shot, made basket will not be equal to no, so the basket is no longer detected. The made basket variable resets to no the next time the player presses the spacebar to throw the basketball.

SAVE POINT

Click the green flag to test the code so far. Shoot some baskets. Make sure that Player 1 Score increases by only 1 point for each basket. Then click the red stop sign and save your program.

THE COMPLETE PROGRAM

Here is the final code. If your program isn't working correctly, check your code against this code.

Cat

Hitbox

Hoop

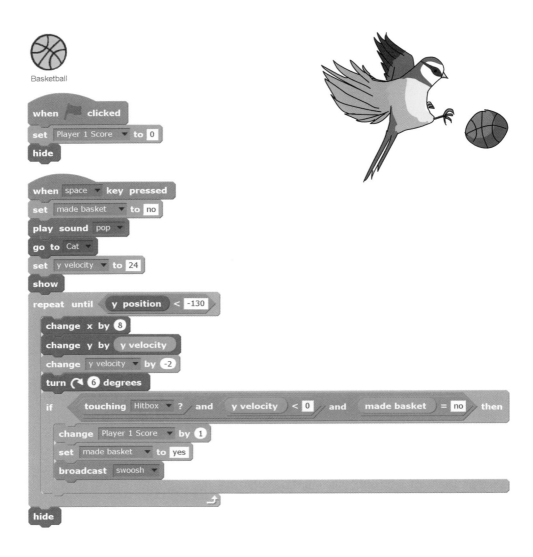

Basketball

```
when [flag] clicked
set Player 1 Score ▼ to 0
hide

when space ▼ key pressed
set made basket ▼ to no
play sound pop ▼
go to Cat ▼
set y velocity ▼ to 24
show
repeat until < y position < -130 >
    change x by 8
    change y by y velocity
    change y velocity ▼ by -2
    turn ↻ 6 degrees
    if < touching Hitbox ▼ ? and y velocity < 0 and made basket = no > then
        change Player 1 Score ▼ by 1
        set made basket ▼ to yes
        broadcast swoosh ▼
hide
```

VERSION 2.0: TWO-PLAYER MODE

Let's upgrade the *Basketball* game by adding a second player. This will be easy since the second player's code will be almost identical to the first player's code.

Duplicate the Cat and Basketball Sprites

Duplicate the Cat sprite and the Basketball sprite by right-clicking them in the Sprite List and selecting **duplicate**. Select the new Cat2 sprite and click the **Costumes** tab at the top of the Blocks Area. Use the Fill tool to make the cat blue.

Then click the **Flip left-right** button at the top-right corner of the Paint Editor to make the second player shoot for the hoop from the other side.

Modify the Code for the Cat2 Sprite

Change the code in the new **Cat2** sprite to match this:

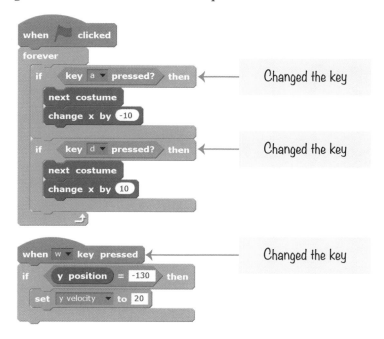

Now two different players will be able to play the game using the same keyboard. Each cat will be controlled by its own unique keys.

Modify the Code for the Basketball2 Sprite

The second player will need their own variable for keeping score. From the orange *Data* category, click the **Make a Variable** button, name the variable Player 2 Score, and select **For all sprites**. Change the code in the new Basketball2 sprite to match the code shown here.

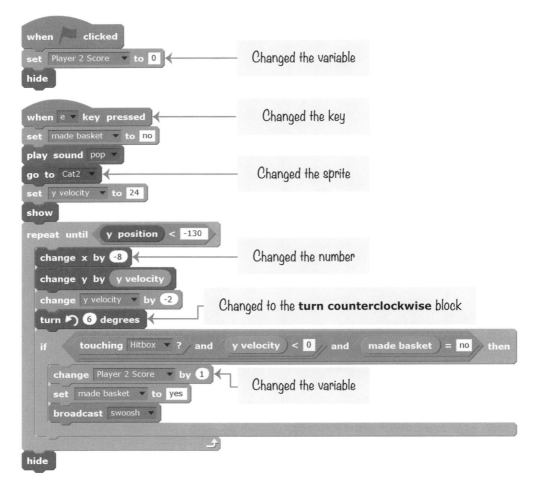

This code makes the basketball thrown by the second player go to the left and assigns the Player 2 Score variable to the second player. You can rename a variable by going to the orange *Data* category, right-clicking the variable, and selecting **Rename variable**.

CHEAT MODE: FREEZE THE HOOP

The moving basketball hoop is a hard target to hit. Let's add a cheat that will freeze it in place for a few seconds when a player presses the 7 key.

Select the Hoop sprite, and click the **Make a Variable** button to create a new For this sprite only variable named freeze. Then modify the code for the Hoop sprite to match the following code.

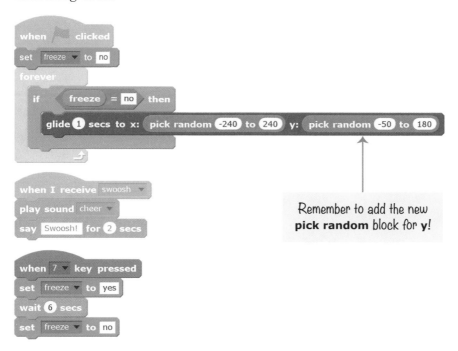

Remember to add the new **pick random** block for **y!**

SAVE POINT

Click the green flag to test the code so far. Press the 7 key, and make sure the hoop stops gliding to new positions for 6 seconds. Then click the red stop sign and save your program.

SUMMARY

In this chapter, you built a game that

▶ Implements gravity and realistic falling

▶ Has a side-view perspective instead of a top-down view

▶ Uses variables to keep track of scores, falling speeds, and the first time a basket is made

▶ Has a hitbox to detect when a basket is made

The use of gravity in this program was pretty simple. By the time you reach Chapter 9, you'll be able to make an advanced platformer game with more complex jumping and falling. But there are plenty of Scratch programming techniques to practice first. In Chapter 5, you'll make a side-view game that uses cloning to duplicate a sprite dozens of times.

REVIEW QUESTIONS

Try to answer the following practice questions to test what you've learned. You probably won't know all the answers off the top of your head, but you can explore the Scratch editor to figure out the answers. (The answers are also online at *http:// www.nostarch.com/scratchplayground/*.)

1. How is a side-view game (like the *Basketball* game) different from a top-down game (like the *Maze Runner* game)?
2. What can a variable store?
3. What is the difference between For this sprite only and For all sprites?
4. How can you make a sprite jump?
5. When the cat jumps in the *Basketball* game, what keeps it from just going up forever?
6. What is the difference between the **glide** and **go to x y** blocks?
7. How do you make the code inside an **if then** block run if *two* conditions are true?

5

A POLISHED BRICK BREAKER GAME

ave you ever seen a brick breaker game? The player controls a paddle at the bottom of the screen to bounce a ball that breaks blocks at the top of the screen. The player loses when the ball gets past the paddle. This game is simple enough to program, but it can look a bit boring. In this chapter, you'll learn a few tricks to make the game more colorful and interesting by adding animations and effects.

You'll use an iterative process: first, you'll make the basic game, and then you'll make small improvements to it. The result will be a more professional-looking game that other Scratchers on the Scratch website will think looks awesome.

The following figure shows what the *Brick Breaker* game looks like before and after polishing it.

Before you start coding, take a look at the final game at *https://www.nostarch.com/scratchplayground/*.

SKETCH OUT THE DESIGN

Let's start by drawing what the game should look like. The sketch for *Brick Breaker* might look something like the following figure.

Score: 0

D Make clones of the brick.

E Make the ball bounce off bricks.

A Make a paddle that moves left and right.

C Make the ball bounce off the paddle.

B Make a ball that bounces off the walls.

F Make "You Win" and "Game Over" messages.

If you want to save time, you can start from the skeleton project file, named *brickbreaker-skeleton.sb2*, in the resources ZIP file. Go to *https://www.nostarch.com/scratchplayground/* and download the ZIP file to your computer by right-clicking the link and selecting **Save link as** or **Save target as**. Extract all the files from the ZIP file. The skeleton project file has all the sprites already loaded, so you'll only need to drag the code blocks into each sprite.

A MAKE A PADDLE THAT MOVES LEFT AND RIGHT

The player will control the paddle by moving the mouse. The ball bounces off the paddle toward the bricks, but the player loses if the ball gets past the paddle.

1. Create the Paddle Sprite

We don't need the orange cat in this game, so right-click the Sprite1 cat in the Sprite List and select **delete** from the menu.

Then paint a sprite by clicking the **Paint new sprite** button next to New sprite. When the Paint Editor appears, draw a wide rectangle using the Rectangle tool.

I've made my paddle green, but you can choose another color. A short paddle makes the ball more difficult to hit. Later, you can experiment with different paddle sizes to make the game easier or harder. Click the ❶ button to open the Info Area, and rename this sprite Paddle.

Next, add this code to program the Paddle sprite to make it follow the mouse along the bottom of the Stage:

The Paddle sprite constantly moves 10 steps directly toward the mouse, but its y position stays set to -140.

Original position   Final position

The paddle's horizontal movement is the result of two moves: moving 10 steps toward the mouse and then setting its y position to -140.

The Paddle sprite will move only left and right because its y position is always set to the bottom of the Stage (-140).

EXPLORE: ROTATION STYLES

The rotation style sets how the sprite looks when it changes direction. The three rotation styles are all around, left-right, and don't rotate.

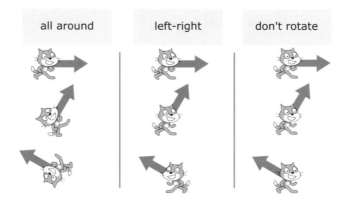

all around   left-right   don't rotate

When a sprite is set to all around, it will face exactly where its direction points. But this won't work for a side-view game (like the *Basketball* game in Chapter 4), because the sprite will be upside down when its direction faces left. Instead, for these games you'll use the left-right rotation style. The sprite will face only 90 degrees (right) or −90 degrees (left), whichever is closest to the sprite's direction. If you don't want the sprite to rotate at all, even as its direction changes, set the rotation style to don't rotate.

Because we're changing the Paddle sprite's direction, we also need to set the sprite's rotation style with the **set rotation style** block. The Paddle sprite is programmed to face and move toward the mouse, but we want the sprite to always look flat and horizontal, so the rotation style is set to don't rotate.

SAVE POINT

Click the green flag to test the code so far. Move the mouse around and see if the Paddle sprite follows it. Make sure the Paddle stays at the bottom of the Stage. Then click the red stop sign and save your program.

B MAKE A BALL THAT BOUNCES OFF THE WALLS

The Scratch Sprite Library has several sprites you could use for the ball, but let's use the Tennis Ball sprite for this game.

2. Create the Tennis Ball Sprite

Click the **Choose sprite from library** button next to New sprite, and select the Tennis Ball sprite from the Sprite Library window. Add the following code:

```
when [flag] clicked
go to x: 0 y: 0
point in direction 135 ▼
wait 1 secs
forever
    move 10 steps
    if on edge, bounce
```

When the game starts, the Tennis Ball sprite starts at position (0, 0) in the center of the Stage; then the Tennis Ball sprite points down and to the right toward the Paddle sprite. Next, in the **forever** loop, the Tennis Ball sprite starts to move. When the Tennis Ball sprite touches the edge of the Stage, it will bounce in a new direction.

SAVE POINT

Click the green flag to test the code so far. Make sure the Tennis Ball sprite moves around and bounces off the edges. The tennis ball will not bounce off the paddle, because you haven't added that code yet. Click the red stop sign and save your program.

ⓒ MAKE THE BALL BOUNCE OFF THE PADDLE

The Tennis Ball sprite now bounces off the walls but not off the Paddle sprite. Let's add that code now.

3. Add the Bounce Code to the Tennis Ball Sprite

Add the following code to the Tennis Ball sprite so it will bounce off the Paddle sprite. To do so, you'll need to create a new broadcast message, bounce.

You'll use the broadcast message in script ❶ to control what happens when the ball touches the paddle in script ❷.

The **point in direction 180 - direction** code in script ❷ might seem a bit mysterious, but this simple equation calculates the direction in which the ball will bounce based on the ball's current direction. If the ball is pointed up and right (45 degrees), then when it bounces off the bottom of a brick, its new direction will be down and right (135 degrees, because $180 - 45 = 135$). If the ball is pointed up and left (-45 degrees), then when it bounces off the bottom of a brick, its new direction will be down and left (225 degrees, because $180 - (-45) = 225$).

You'll use this broadcast message again later in the program when you add code to make the ball bounce off the bricks.

EXPLORE: CLONING

The **create clone of myself** block makes a duplicate of the sprite, which is called a *clone*. This feature is handy whenever you want to create many copies of an object in your game, such as a lot of bad guys that look the same, a bunch of coins for the player to collect, or in the *Brick Breaker* game, the bricks you need to hit.

Let's look at how clones work. Open Scratch in a new tab, and create a new program. Add this code to the Cat sprite:

Script ❶ makes the Cat sprite bounce around the Stage, just like the Tennis Ball sprite does in the *Brick Breaker* game. But in script ❷, we create a clone again and again, every 2 seconds. Script ❸ uses the **when I start as a clone** block to control the behavior of the cloned sprites. What do you think will happen when you run this code? Run the code now to find out if you were right.

The original Cat sprite bounces around the Stage. Every 2 seconds a duplicate of the sprite is created: these are the clones. Each clone will then start to turn because of script ❸.

D MAKE CLONES OF THE BRICK

Now the game needs lots of bricks, so you'll create one Brick sprite and then clone it using Scratch's **create clone** block.

4. Add the Brick Sprite

Click the **Choose sprite from library** button next to New sprite, and select the Button 2 sprite from the Sprite Library window. Click the ❶ button to open the Info Area, and rename this sprite Brick.

You'll have to create a new variable by selecting the orange *Data* category and clicking the **Make a Variable** button. Name this variable Score, and set it to **For all sprites**. Then add the following code to the Brick sprite:

At the beginning of the game, the Score variable is set to 0 so that any points from a previous game are reset. The original sprite hides itself with the **hide** block, shrinks in size by 50 percent, and moves to the top-left corner of the Stage at (−200, 140). The clones, which we'll create next, show themselves with the **show** block.

5. Clone the Brick Sprite

For the *Brick Breaker* game, we want many rows of bricks. To make the rows of bricks, we'll move the original sprite across the top of the screen, creating a trail of clones. Add the following code to the Brick sprite. (Be sure not to confuse the **set x to** and **change x by** blocks!)

```
when [flag] clicked
hide
set [Score ▼] to [0]
set size to (50) %
go to x: (-200) y: (140)
repeat (4)
    repeat (7)
        create clone of [myself ▼]
        change x by (65)
    set x to (-200)
    change y by (-30)
```

This code will create clones of the Brick sprite for all the
bricks in the game, as shown here:

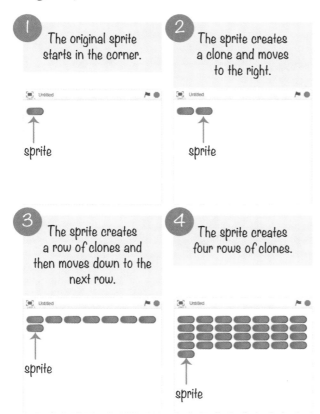

1 The original sprite starts in the corner.

sprite

2 The sprite creates a clone and moves to the right.

sprite

3 The sprite creates a row of clones and then moves down to the next row.

sprite

4 The sprite creates four rows of clones.

sprite

The original sprite moves to the top-left corner of the Stage at (−200, 140) ❶. Then the **repeat 7** block repeatedly moves 65 steps to the right while making clones of itself ❷ to create a row of seven Brick clones ❸. The **repeat 4** block repeats the row-creating code to create four rows of Brick clones ❹. Seven Brick clones multiplied by four rows results in 28 Brick clones. The 29th Brick in the previous figure is the original sprite, not a clone, and we'll hide it next.

After all the clones have been created, the original sprite hides itself. Now all the bricks on the Stage are clones, so you don't need to duplicate the code under the **when I start as a clone** block for the original sprite.

Imagine if you duplicated the sprites instead of cloning them. Then, if you wanted to change the code, you'd have to change all 28 Brick sprites. Cloning saves you a lot of time!

Ⓔ MAKE THE BALL BOUNCE OFF BRICKS

The Tennis Ball sprite bounces off the Stage edges and the Paddle sprite. Now let's make it bounce off the Brick clones.

6. Add the Bounce Code to the Brick Sprite

Update the code for the Brick sprite to match this:

```
when I start as a clone
show
forever
    if   touching Tennis Ball ▼ ?   then
        broadcast bounce ▼
        change Score ▼ by ❶
        delete this clone
```

When the Tennis Ball sprite hits a Brick sprite, the Brick sprite broadcasts the bounce message, which brings the Tennis Ball code into play. The ball's direction changes, just like it does when it hits the paddle. The program adds 1 to the player's Score, and then the clone deletes itself.

SAVE POINT

Click the green flag to test the code so far. Make sure the top part of the Stage fills with Brick clones and the clones disappear when the Tennis Ball sprite bounces off them. Then click the red stop sign and save your program.

F MAKE "YOU WIN" AND "GAME OVER" MESSAGES

You need two more sprites for this game, but they won't appear until the game ends. I created mine with the Paint Editor's Text tool. If the player breaks all the Brick clones, the program displays the You Win sprite. If the tennis ball gets past the paddle, the program displays the Game Over sprite.

7. Modify the Tennis Ball Sprite's Code

When the Tennis Ball sprite gets past the Paddle sprite—that is, when the Tennis Ball sprite's **y position** is less than -140—the game is over. Once the game ends, the Tennis Ball sprite should broadcast a game over message. Add the following code to the Tennis Ball sprite. This will require you to create the game over broadcast message.

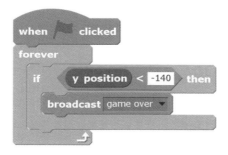

The game over broadcast will tell the Game Over sprite to appear. Let's create the sprite next.

8. Create the Game Over Sprite

Click the **Paint new sprite** button next to New sprite. When the Paint Editor appears, use the Text tool to write *GAME OVER* in red.

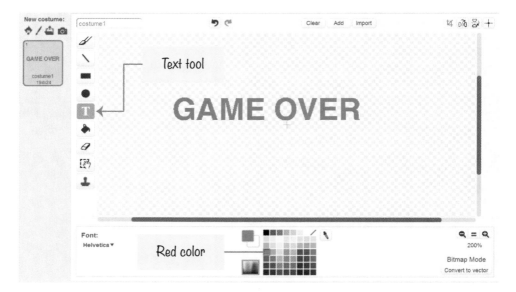

Click the ❶ button to open the Info Area, and rename this sprite Game Over. Then add this code to the Game Over sprite:

The sprite stays hidden until it receives the game over broadcast. The **stop all** block then stops all the sprites from moving as well.

SAVE POINT

Click the green flag to test the code so far. Let the tennis ball fall past the paddle, and make sure the Game Over sprite appears and the program stops. Save your program.

9. Create the You Win Sprite

Click the **Paint new sprite** button next to New sprite. In the Paint Editor, use the Text tool to write *You win!* in green.

Click the ❶ button to open the Info Area, and rename this sprite You Win. Add this code to the You Win sprite:

```
when [flag] clicked
go to x: 0 y: 0
hide
set Score ▼ to 0
wait until Score = 28
show
stop all ▼
```

As with the Game Over sprite, the You Win sprite is hidden until a condition is met. In this game, the player needs to break all 28 bricks to win, so the condition is **Score = 28**. After the You Win sprite displays, the program stops all the other sprites from moving with **stop all**.

SAVE POINT

Click the green flag to test the code so far. Make sure the You Win sprite appears after breaking all the bricks and the program stops. To make winning the game faster, temporarily change the **wait until Score = 28** block to **wait until Score = 1**. Then you only need to break one brick to win. Save your program.

THE COMPLETE PROGRAM

The final code for the entire program is shown here. If your program isn't working right, check your code against this code.

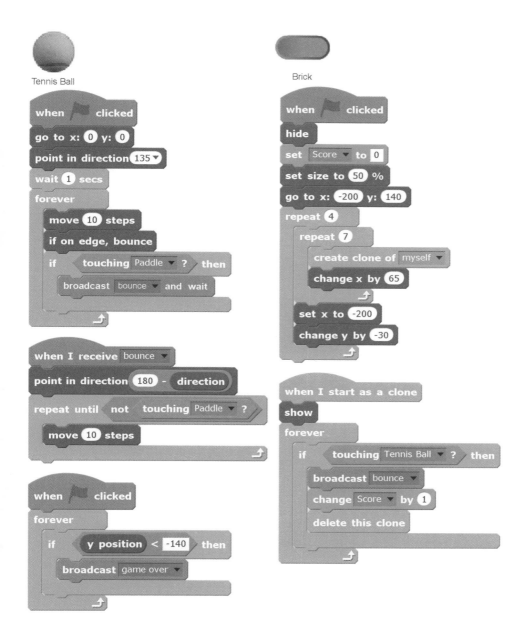

Tennis Ball

```
when [flag] clicked
go to x: 0 y: 0
point in direction 135 ▼
wait 1 secs
forever
    move 10 steps
    if on edge, bounce
    if < touching Paddle ▼ ? > then
        broadcast bounce ▼ and wait
```

```
when I receive bounce ▼
point in direction 180 - direction
repeat until < not < touching Paddle ▼ ? >>
    move 10 steps
```

```
when [flag] clicked
forever
    if < y position < -140 > then
        broadcast game over ▼
```

Brick

```
when [flag] clicked
hide
set Score ▼ to 0
set size to 50 %
go to x: -200 y: 140
repeat 4
    repeat 7
        create clone of myself ▼
        change x by 65
    set x to -200
    change y by -30
```

```
when I start as a clone
show
forever
    if < touching Tennis Ball ▼ ? > then
        broadcast bounce ▼
        change Score ▼ by 1
        delete this clone
```

VERSION 2.0: POLISHING TIME

The game works well as it is. But now you'll add some polish
to the game. Many of the ideas for the polished features in the
Brick Breaker game came from a Nordic Game Indie Night

presentation called "Juice It or Lose It!" by Martin Jonasson and Petri Purho. The word *juice* in game design means *polish*, or modifying a game in small ways to make it feel more alive and responsive. These tricks can turn a barebones game into an exciting, colorful one. A juicy game looks more professional than a plain game. You can watch their presentation where they add juice to their brick breaker game at *https://www .nostarch.com/scratchplayground/*.

You can add many tricks to the *Brick Breaker* game to make it look polished. Even better, you can use these tricks in any of your games. Before you start coding, take a look at the complete program at *https://www.nostarch.com/ scratchplayground/*.

Draw a Cool Backdrop

Adding an interesting background is a simple way to make the game look cooler. Click the Stage in the Sprite List, and then click the **Backdrops** tab above the Blocks Area. In the Paint Editor, select two different purple colors. First, click a light purple color; then click the Color switcher and click a dark purple color. Using the Fill tool's various gradient settings, randomly click around the Paint Editor to create an unusual but interesting background like the one shown in the following figure.

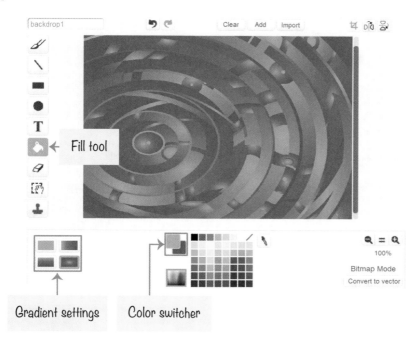

Add Music

Sounds set the mood and make a game feel more alive. With the Stage selected in the Sprite List, click the **Sounds** tab at the top of the Blocks Area. Click the **Choose sound from library** button (it looks like a speaker) under New sound. When the Sound Library window appears, select the dance celebrate sound and click **OK**.

Then click the **Scripts** tab and add this code to the Stage's Scripts Area to give the game some background music:

Make the Paddle Flash When Hit

In this step, you'll make the paddle flash different colors when it is hit by the ball. Add the following code to the Paddle sprite.

The bounce message is broadcast when the Tennis Ball sprite bounces off a Brick clone and when it bounces off the Paddle sprite. The **if distance to Tennis Ball < 60** block makes the color changes happen when the Tennis Ball sprite bounces off the Paddle sprite (which means the ball will be less than 60 steps away).

SAVE POINT

Click the green flag to test the code so far. Make sure the paddle flashes different colors when the ball bounces off it. Then click the red stop sign and save your program.

Add an Animated Entrance and Exit to the Bricks

The Brick clones' entrance to the game is rather boring. They just appear as soon as they're cloned. To animate their entrance, modify the Brick sprite's code to match this code.

```
when I start as a clone
change y by -10
set ghost ▼ effect to 100
show
repeat 10
    change y by 1
    change ghost ▼ effect by -10
    wait 0.01 secs
forever
    if       touching Tennis Ball ▼ ? then
        broadcast bounce ▼
        change Score ▼ by 1
        delete this clone
```

Setting the **ghost effect** to 100 and then slowly decreasing it makes the Brick clones fade into view rather than instantly appear. The code also sets the Brick clones 10 steps below their final positions and slowly raises them by changing their y position in the **repeat** block. This makes the Brick clones look like they're sliding into place.

Click the green flag to test the code so far. Make sure the Brick clones fade into view rather than just instantly appearing. Then click the red stop sign and save your program.

Now let's animate the exit of the Brick clones. Modify the Brick sprite's code so the Brick clones have an animated exit instead of just instantly disappearing.

```
when I start as a clone
change y by -10
set ghost effect to 100
show
repeat 10
    change y by 1
    change ghost effect by -10
    wait 0.01 secs
forever
    if touching Tennis Ball ? then
        broadcast bounce
        change Score by 1
        repeat 10
            change color effect by 25
            change ghost effect by 5
            change size by -4
            change y by 4
            turn ↺ 15 degrees
        delete this clone
```

Now the Brick clones will disappear in an exciting way! The **change effect by** blocks inside the **repeat** loop will make the Brick clones flash different colors and increase their ghost effect so they become more and more transparent. Meanwhile, the **change size by -4** block causes the Brick clones to shrink, the **change y by 4** block lifts them up, and the **turn clockwise 15 degrees** block rotates them. This animated exit is short but fun to watch.

SAVE POINT

Click the green flag to test the code so far. Hit the bricks with the tennis ball, and make sure they spin and move up as they fade out of sight rather than just instantly disappearing. Then click the red stop sign and save your program.

Add a Sound Effect to the Brick Exit

Let's also make the Brick clones play different sound effects as they disappear. Select the Brick sprite in the Sprite List, and then click the **Sounds** tab above the Blocks Area. Click the **Choose sound from library** button under New sound, and select laser1 from the Sound Library. Repeat this step to add the laser2 sound as well.

Modify the Brick sprite's code to match this code:

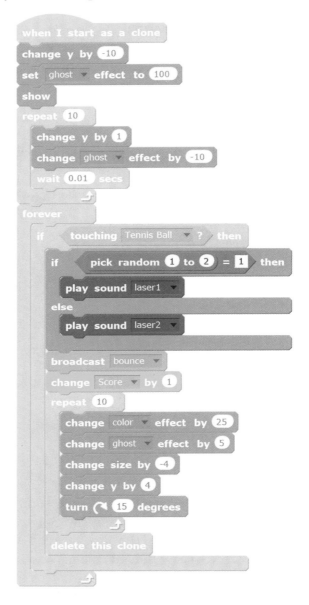

When these sounds have been loaded and the following code has been added, the Brick clones will play a random sound effect as they disappear. The **if then else** block adds some variety to the program's sound effects by randomly selecting which sound to play. Each time the Tennis Ball sprite touches a Brick clone, the program will choose either 1 or 2 at random and then play a different sound as a result.

Add a Sound Effect to the Tennis Ball

Now you'll add a sound effect for when the Tennis Ball sprite hits the Paddle sprite. The pop sound is already loaded for each sprite; all you have to do is update the Tennis Ball sprite's code to match this:

```
when [flag] clicked
go to x: 0 y: 0
point in direction 135 ▼
wait 1 secs
forever
    move 10 steps
    if on edge, bounce
    if < touching Paddle ▼ ? > then
        play sound pop ▼
        broadcast bounce ▼
```

Add a Trail Behind the Tennis Ball

Adding a trail of clones behind the Tennis Ball sprite as it moves around the Stage will give it a cool comet tail. You don't want to use clones of the Tennis Ball sprite, because they would respond to the bounce broadcast whenever the original Tennis Ball sprite bounces. Instead, click the **Choose sprite from library** button next to New sprite. Then select **Tennis**

Ball from the Sprite Library window to create another sprite called Tennis Ball2. You'll clone this second ball to create the trail. Unlike a Tennis Ball clone, the Tennis Ball2 clones won't have a **when I receive bounce** block. Add this code to the Tennis Ball2 sprite:

```
when [flag] clicked          when I start as a clone
hide                         show
                             go to [Tennis Ball ▼]
                             repeat 15
                                 change size by -4
                                 change [ghost ▼] effect by 5
                             delete this clone
```

The only thing the clone is programmed to do is go to the current Tennis Ball sprite's location. The tennis ball keeps moving, but the clone stays in place, shrinking and becoming more transparent. At the end of this shrinking and fading animation, the clone is deleted.

You'll also need to update the Tennis Ball sprite with this code:

```
when [flag] clicked
go to front
forever
    wait 0.1 secs
    create clone of [Tennis Ball2 ▼]
```

This script makes a new Tennis Ball2 clone after a 0.1 second wait, which creates the trail of tennis balls.

SAVE POINT

Click the green flag to test the code so far. Make sure a trail of shrinking Tennis Ball2 clones follows the original Tennis Ball sprite. Then click the red stop sign and save your program.

Add an Animated Entrance for the Game Over Sprite

When the player loses, the *GAME OVER* text simply appears. It would be more exciting if the *GAME OVER* text had an animated entrance like the Brick clones do. Modify the Game Over sprite's code to match the following code. First load the gong sound effect by clicking the **Choose sound from library** button on the Sounds tab. You'll create a new broadcast message named stop game that will tell the Paddle and Tennis Ball sprites to stop moving.

At the start of the game, the Game Over sprite hides itself and sets its ghost effect to 100. When the **show** block runs at the end of the game, the *GAME OVER* text is still completely invisible. The animation code inside the **repeat 10** block makes the *GAME OVER* text slowly fade in by changing the ghost effect by -10. The **turn clockwise 15 degrees** and **change size by 12** blocks rotate and enlarge the text. After a 4 second pause, the **stop all** block ends the program.

To handle the stop game broadcast message in the Tennis Ball and Paddle sprites, add the following code to *both* of these sprites:

Add this code to the Tennis Ball and Paddle sprites.

The reason you need to use the **stop other scripts in sprite** block instead of **stop all** is that the program needs to continue running while the *GAME OVER* text is animated. The **stop other scripts in sprite** block will stop the Tennis Ball and Paddle sprites from moving but let the other sprites in the program continue running. When the Game Over sprite has finished appearing on the screen, the **stop all** block will end the entire program.

SAVE POINT

Click the green flag to test the code so far. Try to lose the game, and make sure the *GAME OVER* text has an animated entrance instead of just instantly appearing on the screen. Then click the red stop sign and save your program.

Add an Animated Entrance for the You Win Sprite

Let's give the You Win sprite a fancy, animated entrance too. Update the code in the You Win sprite to match the following. You will have to load the sound effect named gong by clicking the **Choose sound from library** button on the Sounds tab.

```
when ⚑ clicked
go to x: 0 y: 0
hide
set ghost ▾ effect to 100
set size to 100 %
set Score ▾ to 0
wait until ⟨ Score = 28 ⟩
play sound gong ▾
broadcast stop game ▾
show
repeat 10
    change ghost ▾ effect by -10
    change size by 3
    change y by 4
    wait 0.01 secs
    ↺
wait 0.2 secs
repeat 2
    set brightness ▾ effect to 50
    wait 0.1 secs
    set brightness ▾ effect to 0
    wait 0.1 secs
    ↺
wait 4 secs
stop all ▾
```

There are two sets of animations, one in the **repeat 10** block and another in the **repeat 2** block. The code in the **repeat 10** block makes the You Win sprite fade into visibility, enlarges it, and moves it upward. After this short animation plays, the **repeat 2** block's code increases the sprite's brightness to 50, waits a tenth of a second, and then resets the brightness to 0. This makes the sprite look like it's flashing. After a 4 second pause, the **stop all** block ends the program.

Click the green flag to test the code so far. When you win the game, make sure the *You win!* text has an animated entrance instead of just instantly appearing on the screen. To make winning the game faster, temporarily change the **wait until Score = 28** block to **wait until Score = 1**. Then you need to break only one brick to win. Save your program.

SUMMARY

In this chapter, you built a game that

- ▶ Uses clones to quickly create many copies of the Brick sprite and a trail of Tennis Ball2 sprites

- ▶ Controls the Paddle sprite with the mouse instead of the keyboard arrow keys

- ▶ Shows the player *GAME OVER* and *You Win!* messages that you created using the Paint Editor's Text tool

- ▶ Has several animated entrances and exits for sprites

- ▶ Uses sound effects and background music to make the game feel more alive

Making the *Brick Breaker* game provided you with several techniques that you can add to future games. You can include animated entrances, color flashes, and sound effects in many programs to make them more exciting and fun. But it's always best to make sure the plain, basic version of your game is working first and then start making it look cooler later.

This chapter also introduced cloning, which is a useful technique that we will use in the *Snaaaaaake* game in Chapter 6. As you read on, the games you create will become more sophisticated, but don't worry: you just have to keep following the instructions step-by-step!

REVIEW QUESTIONS

Try to answer the following practice questions to test what you've learned. You probably won't know all the answers off the top of your head, but you can explore the Scratch editor to figure out the answers. (The answers are also at the back of this book.)

1. How does the program know when the Tennis Ball sprite has gotten past the Paddle sprite?
2. Which block creates clones of a sprite?
3. Which block has the code that clones run when they are created?
4. What are the three rotation styles?
5. Why do the You Win and Game Over sprites hide themselves after you click the green flag?
6. What does the **wait until** block do?

6
SNAAAAAAKE!

he snake game, or *Snaaaaaake*, is a remake of a popular game that many people have played on their phones or calculators. You might know this game by another name—*Nibbles* or *Worm*. To play, you use the arrow keys to direct a constantly moving snake toward apples that appear on the screen.

The more apples the snake eats, the longer the snake gets and the harder it becomes to keep the snake from crashing into itself or the edges of the Stage. You can't slow down the snake, and the game is over when the snake crashes.

Before you start coding, take a look at the final program at *https://www.nostarch.com/scratchplayground/*.

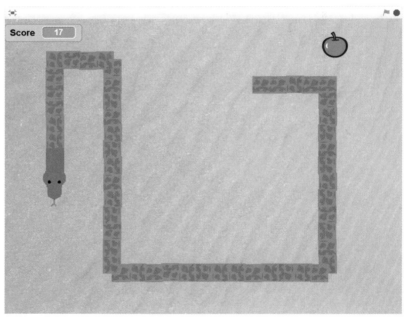

Even though the snake grows pretty long, you still have to measure it in inches, because snakes don't have feet! (I make no apology for the corny snake jokes in this chapter; I think they're hiss-terical.)

SKETCH OUT THE DESIGN

Let's sketch what the game should look like.

If you want to save time, you can start from the skeleton project file, named *snake-skeleton.sb2*, in the resources ZIP file. Go to *https://www.nostarch.com/scratchplayground/* and download the ZIP file to your computer by right-clicking the link and selecting **Save link as** or **Save target as**. Extract all the files from the ZIP file. The skeleton project file has all the sprites already loaded, so you'll only need to drag the code blocks into each sprite.

Ⓐ MAKE A SNAKE HEAD THAT MOVES AROUND

We'll start by creating a snake head that the player can control with the keyboard. The arrow keys will change the snake head's direction, but the snake's head will always move forward. We'll program the snake's body later.

1. Create the Head Sprite

First, let's make the background more interesting. Click
the Stage in the Sprite List,
and then click the **Backdrops**
tab above the Blocks Area.
Click the **Upload backdrop
from file** button under New
backdrop, and select *sand.jpg*
from the resources ZIP file.

Next, draw the snake's
head. Click the **Paint new
sprite** button next to New
sprite. In the Paint Editor,
draw a top-down view of a snake head that faces right. Since
all Scratch sprites start facing 90 degrees (that is, to the
right), you should draw the head facing right. After drawing
it, rename the sprite Head.

Use the Shrink tool or Grow tool at the top of the Scratch
editor to shrink or grow your Head sprite. The Head sprite
should be about as big as in the following picture.

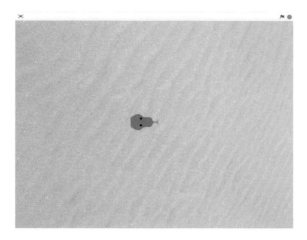

Add this code to the Head sprite:

Script ❶ sets the starting position and the starting direction (0 degrees, or straight up) for the snake head. It sets the player's score to 0, which will require you to create a For all sprites variable named Score. As in previous projects, you can create a variable by clicking the **Make a Variable** button in the orange *Data* category. Because we want the snake to *never* stop moving, program ❶ includes a **forever move 10 steps** loop.

Scripts ❷, ❸, ❹, and ❺ are short scripts that handle the player's controls: the directions correspond to the up, down, left, and right arrow keys.

Click the green flag to test the code so far. Make sure the arrow keys correctly direct the snake head in all four directions: up, down, left, and right. Then click the red stop sign and save your program.

EXPLORE: WHEN KEY PRESSED VS. IF KEY PRESSED? THEN

In this *Snaaaaaake* program, the **when key pressed** code block moves the player around and is used when a key is supposed to be *pressed once*.

In the maze game in Chapter 3, the **if then** block with a **key pressed?** block inside a **forever** loop moved the player around. Use the **if key pressed? then** code when a key is meant to be *pressed and held down*.

Snake code   Maze code

These two ways of programming the player's controls are not quite the same. Be sure to use the appropriate code blocks for the game you want to make. Because the snake is always moving, the player needs to press a key only once to change the snake's direction. This is why the *Snaaaaaake* game uses the **when key pressed** blocks.

Ⓑ MAKE APPLES APPEAR

The basics of moving the snake around are done, so let's add the apple the snake will try to eat.

2. Add the Apple Sprite

Click the **Choose sprite from library** button next to New sprite, and select the Apple sprite from the Sprite Library. Add this code:

```
when [flag] clicked
set size to (50) %
forever
    if < touching [Head ▼] ? > then
        change [Score ▼] by (1)
        go to x: (pick random (-220) to (220)) y: (pick random (-160) to (160))
```

This code makes the Apple sprite disappear when the snake touches it and then reappear elsewhere on the Stage. The new position is picked from random numbers, like rolling dice. The script also adds 1 to the Score variable each time the Head sprite touches the Apple sprite.

SAVE POINT

Click the green flag to test the code so far. Move the snake around to eat the apple. When the snake's head touches the apple, make sure the apple moves somewhere else. The Score variable should increase by 1 each time the snake's head touches the apple. Then click the red stop sign and save your program.

Ⓒ MAKE A BODY THAT APPEARS BEHIND THE SNAKE HEAD

Next, we'll add the body of the snake, which we want to grow with each apple it eats.

3. Create the Body Sprite

Click the **Paint new sprite** button next to New sprite to create a new sprite. Draw a small square using the same color as the snake's head. Make sure the costume center is in the middle of the square by clicking the **Set costume center** button and then clicking the middle of the square.

Click the sprite's ❶ button to open its Info Area, and rename the sprite Body.

4. Create the Body Sprite's Second Costume

While you're still in the Paint Editor, right-click the costume1 costume, and select **duplicate** from the menu. Using the Fill tool, change the color of the square to a different color, such as a light green. (My program uses dark green for the snake's head and a lighter green for the body's second costume.) We'll use the light green color to detect whether the snake has crashed into itself. You can also add some patterns on top of this color.

You can draw clothes on the snake's body if you want. I'd recommend a boa-tie, a feather boa, or some Nike snake-ers. Or you can leave it s-naked. (Will these snake puns ever end? Don't asp me!)

Just make sure the Body costumes are square and that costume2 uses a different color than costume1 and the Head sprite!

5. Add the Code for the Body Sprite

Click the **Scripts** tab, and add the following code to the Body sprite. We want the Body sprite to always follow the Head sprite and generate clones of itself.

The original Body sprite code runs under the **when green flag clicked** block in script ❶. As the Head sprite moves around the Stage, the Body sprite creates a trail of Body clones in its path.

The Body clones code runs under **when I start as a clone** in script ❷. When the Body clone is first created, it points in a random direction. The **pick random 0 to 3 * 90** block makes the Body clone face 0, 90, 180, or 270 degrees. This rotation makes the body segments look slightly different.

The clones eventually need to delete themselves from the Stage so that the snake doesn't just keep growing longer. So each clone waits for a short time based on the Score variable in the **wait Score / 5 secs** block before deleting itself. Every clone waits this amount of time, so the first Body clones made are the first Body clones deleted.

Eating apples increases the Score variable. As the Score variable increases, the amount of time a Body clone waits before deleting itself also increases. This longer wait makes the snake look longer, because more Body clones remain on the Stage. So the more apples the snake eats, the longer the snake gets.

When Score is set to 0, the wait is 0/5 seconds, or 0 seconds. When Score is set to 1, the wait is 1/5, or 0.2 seconds. When Score is 2, the wait is 2/5, or 0.4 seconds. Each point added to Score adds another 0.2 seconds of wait time, resulting in a longer and longer snake. As the snake gets longer, the difficulty of the game really scales up!

6. Detect Whether the Snake Crashes into Itself or a Wall

When the snake crashes into itself or the edges of the Stage, we want to run the **when I receive game over** code: the Head sprite will say "Ouch!" for 2 seconds and then stop the program. Instead of writing the same code twice, let's put the code for all crashes under a **when I receive game over** block so that either crash can broadcast game over and run this code. If you want to change the code, you just need to change it in one place—in the **when I receive game over** script.

Add the following code to the Head sprite:

```
when [flag] clicked
go to x: 0 y: -100
point in direction 0 ▾
set Score ▾ to 0
forever
  move 10 steps
  if < touching color [ ] ? > then
    broadcast game over ▾ and wait
  if < touching edge ▾ ? > then
    broadcast game over ▾ and wait
```

```
when I receive game over ▾
say Ouch! for 2 secs
stop all ▾
```

Using the **touching color?** block, the first **if** loop tests for the condition when the snake touches its own body: make sure you use the color you used in costume2 for this condition. The next two **if** statements test the horizontal and vertical boundaries of the Stage. When the snake crosses them, the same game over broadcast is sent. Let's hope the player is quick enough to avoid crashing; otherwise, that snake is hiss-tory!

Did you notice the **wait 0.01 secs** block in the Body sprite that makes the Body clones wait a bit before changing costumes? Here's the code for the Body sprite again:

```
when [flag] clicked
switch costume to costume1
forever
    go to Head
    wait 0.01 secs          ← Added a slight pause
    create clone of myself
```

The second costume for the Body sprite has the lighter color that the Head sprite uses to detect if the snake has crashed into itself. Because the Body clones are created at the same place as the Head sprite, they are touching the Head when they first appear. This is why we want to pause the crash detection when the clone is created. Without this pause, the Head sprite would think it crashed into the Body clone that was just created because it was touching the lighter color.

SAVE POINT

Click the green flag to test the code so far. Crash into the wall and into the snake's body on purpose to make sure the crash detection works. If your snake appears to be crashing even though it is not touching itself or the edges, try increasing the wait time from 0.01 to 0.02 or larger. Also make sure that the game over code *doesn't* run if the snake isn't crashing into anything. Then click the red stop sign and save your program.

THE COMPLETE PROGRAM

The final code for the entire program is shown here. If your program isn't working correctly, check it against this code.

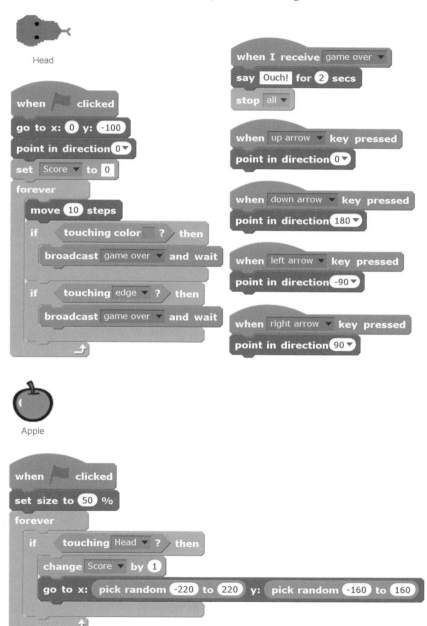

Head

```
when [flag] clicked
go to x: 0 y: -100
point in direction 0 ▾
set Score ▾ to 0
forever
    move 10 steps
    if < touching color [ ] ? > then
        broadcast game over ▾ and wait
    if < touching edge ▾ ? > then
        broadcast game over ▾ and wait
```

```
when I receive game over ▾
say Ouch! for 2 secs
stop all ▾
```

```
when up arrow ▾ key pressed
point in direction 0 ▾
```

```
when down arrow ▾ key pressed
point in direction 180 ▾
```

```
when left arrow ▾ key pressed
point in direction -90 ▾
```

```
when right arrow ▾ key pressed
point in direction 90 ▾
```

Apple

```
when [flag] clicked
set size to 50 %
forever
    if < touching Head ▾ ? > then
        change Score ▾ by 1
        go to x: pick random -220 to 220 y: pick random -160 to 160
```

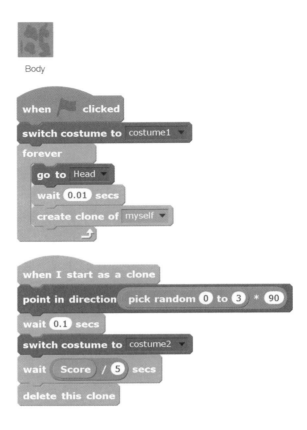

Body

```
when 🚩 clicked
switch costume to costume1 ▾
forever
    go to Head ▾
    wait 0.01 secs
    create clone of myself ▾
```

```
when I start as a clone
point in direction (pick random 0 to 3) * 90
wait 0.1 secs
switch costume to costume2 ▾
wait (Score / 5) secs
delete this clone
```

VERSION 2.0: ADD BONUS FRUIT

Just having one type of goal in a game can get boring after a while. Let's add some bonus fruit!

Let's add a second type of fruit that will increase the score by 3 points when the snake eats it. Click the **Choose sprite from library** button. From the Sprite Library window, select **Fruit Platter** and click **OK**. (Or maybe choose a dessert instead if your snake is a pie-thon.)

Add this code to the new sprite:

```
when [flag] clicked
hide
set size to (50) %
forever
    wait (10) secs
    go to x: (pick random (-150) to (150)) y: (pick random (-150) to (150))
    show
```

```
when [flag] clicked
forever
    if <touching [Head ▼] ?> then
        hide
        change [Score ▼] by (3)
```

The Fruit Platter sprite's code is almost identical to the Apple sprite's code except it has a 10-second pause before reappearing somewhere else on the Stage after the snake touches it. With these bonus points, the snake's score will really adder up!

SAVE POINT

Click the green flag to test the code so far. After 10 seconds, the Fruit Platter sprite should appear. Make sure the Score variable increases by 3 points when the snake touches the Fruit Platter sprite and that the sprite then disappears. Then click the red stop sign and save your program.

CHEAT MODE: INVINCIBILITY

It would be fun to make the snake very, very long! Let's add a cheat mode so the snake can keep growing without crashing into itself. We'll also add a rainbow effect to the snake so that the player can see when cheat mode is enabled.

Modify the Head

Modify the Head sprite's code to match the following. You're adding to the script you wrote earlier and adding a whole new script, too. Both will require you to make a new variable named cheat mode. Make this variable For all sprites.

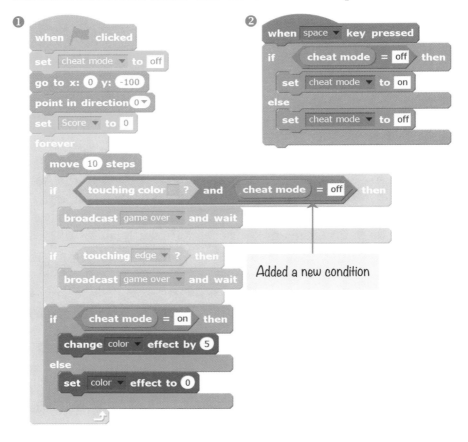

Added a new condition

Script ❷ controls how the cheat mode works. Pressing the spacebar toggles the cheat mode variable between on and off. When set to on, the game over message will not be broadcast, even if the Head is touching the lighter color. The reason is that, in script ❶, you've added **and cheat mode = off** to the **if then** block that checks whether the snake has crashed into itself. If cheat mode is set to on, it doesn't matter if the snake has crashed into itself, because both **touching color?** and **cheat mode = off** must be true before **broadcast game over and wait** runs.

Script ❶ also has an **if then else** block that will give the Head a rainbow effect when the cheat mode is enabled. When the cheat is not enabled, the color effect is reset to 0, which makes the sprite revert to its original color.

Modify the Body Code

Now we want to add this rainbow effect to the Body clones. Modify the Body sprite's code to match this:

```
when [flag] clicked
switch costume to costume1 ▾
forever
    go to Head ▾
    wait 0.01 secs
    create clone of myself ▾
    if < cheat mode = on > then
        change color ▾ effect by 5
    else
        set color ▾ effect to 0
```

When the cheat mode variable is set to on, the Body sprite will gradually change its color effect to produce a rainbow. Otherwise, the Body sprite sets its color effect to 0.

CHEAT MODE: CHOP OFF YOUR TAIL!

The game is no longer a challenge if the snake is invincible. But it would be convenient if you could temporarily get rid of the snake's body if you're about to crash into it. Let's add a cheat that will instantly remove the body.

Add this code to the Body sprite:

When the player presses the C key, all the clones will delete themselves. (Nothing happens to the original sprite because it is not a clone.)

SUMMARY

In this chapter, you built a game that

▶ Uses a sprite to generate a trail of clones as it moves around the Stage

▶ Uses a snake head and body costumes that you drew in the Paint Editor

▶ Detects when the snake head touches the body by checking whether the head is touching the colors on the body

- Uses a variable to track when a cheat mode is turned on or off
- Lets the player control the direction of the snake with the keyboard but not the speed
- Has no end goal; the player continues playing as long as possible

The *Snaaaaaake* game's keyboard controls are similar to those of the *Maze Runner* game in Chapter 3. The player has a top-down view and moves up, down, left, and right. However, the *Snaaaaaake* game is different because the player's character is *always* moving. The player can control only the direction. You can use this style of movement in fast-paced games of your own design.

In Chapter 7, you'll learn how to use the mouse in your programs by creating a clone of the *Fruit Ninja* game. Then your programs will be able to use a keyboard, a mouse, or both!

REVIEW QUESTIONS

Try to answer the following practice questions to test what you've learned. You probably won't know all the answers off the top of your head, but you can explore the Scratch editor to figure out the answers. (The answers are also online at *http://www.nostarch.com/scratchplayground/*.)

1. What is the difference between **when key pressed** blocks and **if key pressed? then** blocks?
2. What does the **go to x: pick random -220 to 220 y: pick random -160 to 160** block do?
3. What is the difference between the **glide** block and the **go to** block?
4. Why do you need to draw the snake head facing to the right?
5. Why does the costume center of the Head sprite need to be set at the center?

7

FRUIT SLICER

Fruit Ninja was a popular mobile game released in 2010. In the game, fruit is thrown in the air, and the player must slice it before it hits the ground. In this chapter, you'll make the *Fruit Slicer* game, which copies the mechanics of the *Fruit Ninja* game. Just as exciting, we'll program this game using some completely new Scratch features, so get ready!

Before you start coding, look at the final program at *https://www.nostarch.com/scratchplayground/*.

In the version we'll create, the player slices fruit by clicking and dragging the mouse.

SKETCH OUT THE DESIGN

Let's draw what the game should look like. The sketch for the *Fruit Slicer* game should look something like this:

E — Make the health sprites.

B — Make the slice trail.

C — Make the begin button.

A — Make the start screen backdrop.

D — Make the fruit and bombs throw themselves.

F — Make the game ending.

If you want to save time, you can start from the skeleton project file, named *fruitslicer-skeleton.sb2*, in the resources ZIP file. Go to *https://www.nostarch.com/scratchplayground/* and download the ZIP file to your computer by right-clicking the link and selecting **Save link as** or **Save target as**. Extract all the files from the ZIP file. The skeleton project file has all the sprites already loaded, so you'll only need to drag the code blocks into each sprite.

Ⓐ MAKE THE START SCREEN BACKDROP

Fruit Slicer will have a *start screen*. When the player clicks the green flag, the start screen shows the game's title. When the player loses, the game will return to the start screen. The start screen is a good place to put your name or logo when you show off your games to others. In fact, try to come up with a game studio name for you and your programs now!

Start a new project in the Scratch editor, and enter *Fruit Slicer* as the project name.

1. Draw the Backdrops

Select the Stage in the Sprite List, and then click the **Backdrops** tab at the top of the Blocks Area. (The Costumes tab is renamed Backdrops when the Stage is selected.) Select a color, and then use the Line tool to draw the letters in the *Fruit Slicer* title. Then use the Fill tool to fill in the letters.

After drawing the title, replace the white background with a dark brown gradient. (When you select the Fill tool, the four gradient buttons appear next to the color buttons.) First click the Color switcher and select a light brown color. Then click one of the gradient buttons to select the gradient type. I used the vertical gradient.

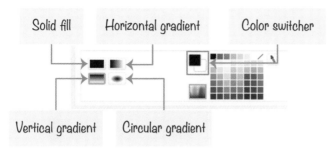

Solid fill Horizontal gradient Color switcher

Vertical gradient Circular gradient

Click the Paint Editor's canvas to fill the background with your gradient. If you want to experiment, click the **Undo** button at the top of the Paint Editor before you try a different gradient. Be sure to also fill in the holes in the *R* letters. When you're done, rename the backdrop start screen.

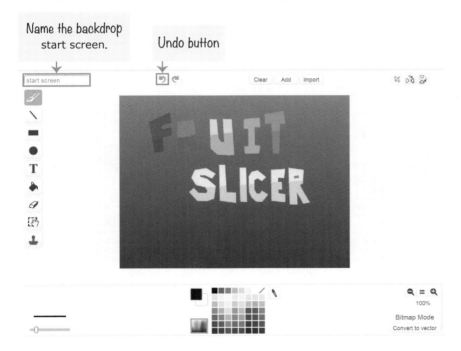

Name the backdrop start screen. Undo button

Now we need to create a plain backdrop. When the game begins, the program should hide the *Fruit Slicer* title and switch to this backdrop. Click the **Paint new backdrop** button under New backdrop to create a second backdrop. Then draw a brown gradient for this backdrop, like this:

Rename this new backdrop game screen. We'll switch between the start screen and game screen backdrops when the game starts.

2. Add the Code for the Stage

Now let's program the Stage. Select the Stage in the Sprite List, and click the **Scripts** tab at the top of the Blocks Area. Create two variables, Score and High Score, by clicking the **Make a Variable** button in the orange *Data* category. Make both variables For all sprites.

NOTE   *The Stage only uses For all sprites variables, so the For this sprite only option won't even appear here!*

You also need to create two new broadcast messages, start screen and start game. Do this by clicking the black triangle in a **broadcast** or **when I receive** block and selecting **new message**. Then add the following scripts to the Stage.

This code resets High Score and Score to 0 when the program begins. The start screen message is broadcast at the beginning of the program and when the player loses a game. The Score variable is reset to 0, and **switch backdrop to start screen** makes the start screen appear again when the player loses a game.

Ⓑ MAKE THE SLICE TRAIL

There isn't a sprite used for the player's character in *Fruit Slicer*. Instead, the player clicks and drags the mouse across the screen, causing a trail to briefly appear as a blade slice effect.

3. Draw the Slice Sprite

Click the **Paint new sprite** button next to New sprite. Open the Info Area and rename the sprite Slice. In the Paint Editor, draw a light blue rectangle that looks like the following.

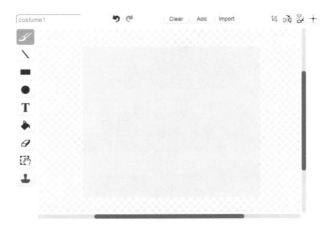

The Slice sprite should *not* be the same color as any color used in the fruits. Otherwise, some of the fruits will end up slicing other fruit.

EXPLORE: MAKING LISTS

Now you'll learn about an advanced Scratch feature—a new way to store data. A *list* is like a variable except it can store many values instead of just one value. Open a new web browser tab and start a new Scratch editor. We will explore the list blocks in a new Scratch project. Select the orange *Data* category and click the **Make a List** button to open the New List window. Name the list example list and make it For all sprites.

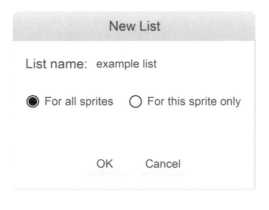

New dark orange blocks will appear under the **Make a List** button.

Lists have more than **set to** and **change by** blocks. Lists have values, but each value also has a *position*, so the values need different kinds of code blocks. Positions in a list are defined by numbers; number 1 is the first value in the list.

The following blocks control lists:

▶ The **add to** block adds a value to the end of the list.

▶ The **delete** block removes the value at a certain position.

▶ The **insert at** block is like the **add to** block, but you can also select the position where the value should be inserted.

▶ The **replace item** block is like a combination of **delete** and **insert at**. It replaces the value at a certain position with a new value.

Add the following code and then double-click it to run it. Take a look at the effects of these code blocks on a list named **example list**.

(continued)

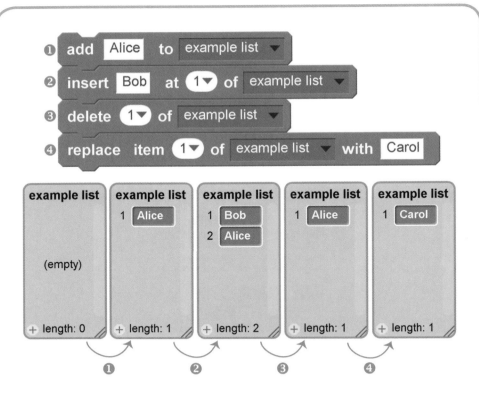

Recall that you can use the value in a variable in its bubble-shaped block. The list's bubble-shaped blocks are similar but require you to specify a position so the bubble-shaped block knows which value in the list it should get. The scripts on the left and right sides both make the cat say "Hello!", but the code that uses a list (left) must also specify the position of the value to use:

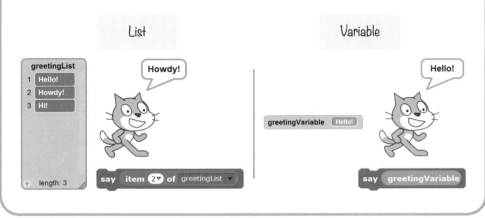

4. Create Lists and Variables for the Slice Sprite

You'll create a list for the *Fruit Slicer* game to keep track of where the player is "slicing" on the screen. Because the slice is drawn between many x and y positions with *Pen* blocks, using a list is ideal.

Click the **Scripts** tab at the top of the Blocks Area, and select the orange *Data* category. Click the **Make a List** button to open the New List window. Name the list slice x and make it For this sprite only.

New dark orange blocks will appear under the Make a List button.

In the orange *Data* category, click the **Make a List** button to make a second list for *Fruit Slicer*. Name the list slice y and make it For this sprite only.

Then click **Make a Variable**, create a variable named i, and make it For this sprite only. You'll use this i variable in the next step. The Slice sprite will use the two lists and i variable to draw the light blue trail.

5. Record the Mouse Movements

You'll use the **Pen** blocks to draw lines for the slice. But first you need to know *where* to draw the lines. Add the following code to the Slice sprite:

```
when [flag] clicked
delete all of slice x
delete all of slice y
forever
    if < mouse down? > then
        add (mouse x) to slice x
        add (mouse y) to slice y
    if < length of slice x > 4  or  not < mouse down? > > then
        delete 1 of slice x
        delete 1 of slice y
```

When the player clicks and holds down the mouse button, the mouse position's x- and y-coordinates are repeatedly added to the end of the slice x and slice y lists. If more than four values are in the lists, the value at the beginning of each list is deleted. This is how the program records the mouse's last four x- and y-coordinates. The first values are also deleted when the mouse button isn't being held down, so the trail shortens when the player releases the mouse button.

This script provides the proper coordinates for the slice x and slice y lists. The next script will actually draw the slice trail.

6. Make a Custom Block to Draw the Slice

Select the purple *More Blocks* category and click the **Make a Block** button to open the New Block window. The purple blocks are custom Scratch blocks that you create.

Fill in the name **draw slice** for your new purple block. Click the gray triangle to expand the Options, and check the **Run without screen refresh** checkbox. With this box checked, Scratch will run the code in your custom purple block in Turbo Mode, even if the player didn't enable Turbo Mode by SHIFT-clicking on the green flag. Click **OK** to create the custom block.

A new **draw slice** block will appear in the dark purple *More Blocks* category.

This new block with the curved top in the Scripts Area is the *defining* block for the **draw slice** block. When you want to use this new defining block, you must also drag the **draw slice** block, which is the *calling* block, from the Blocks Area into the code. Whenever Scratch runs this calling block, the code in the defining block is run.

Add the following code to the Slice sprite:

The color for the **set pen color to** block should be the same color as the blue rectangle Slice sprite. Click the block's color square, and then click the light blue color.

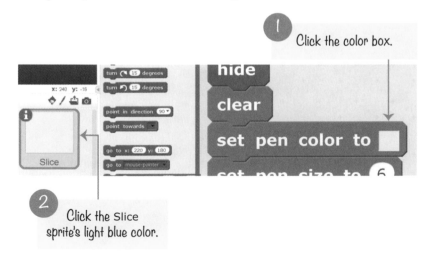

This script hides the Slice sprite and sets the pen to the right size and color. Then the **forever** loop continually runs the **draw slice** block.

Next, you need to define the **define draw slice** block. You want **draw slice** to draw a line starting with the first coordinates: the first value in the slice x list (for the x position) and the first in the slice y list (for the y position). This line goes to the x and y positions in the next values of the slice x and slice y lists, then the next values, and so on, until the last pair of values is reached. Our code will make sure the lengths of the slice x and slice y lists are always the same. Add the following code to the **define draw slice** block. Notice that the length of slice x block is dark orange and from the *Data* category, not the green *Operators* category.

```
define draw slice
clear
if < length of [slice x ▼] > [0] > then
    pen up
    go to x: (item (1▼) of [slice x ▼]) y: (item (1▼) of [slice y ▼])
    pen down
    set [i ▼] to [2]
    repeat until < (i) > (length of [slice x ▼]) >
        go to x: (item (i) of [slice x ▼]) y: (item (i) of [slice y ▼])
        change [i ▼] by (1)
    pen up
```

This code lifts up the pen before moving it to the first x- and y-coordinate values in slice x and slice y and then sets the pen down. Inside the **repeat until** loop, the code uses a temporary variable named i to keep track of where the pen should move next.

The first time through the **repeat until** loop, the sprite moves to value 2 of the slice x and slice y lists. The pen draws a line as the sprite moves. Then i increases by 1 the next time through the loop, and the sprite moves to value 3 of the slice x and slice y lists. The loop continues until i is larger than the number of values in the list (that is, the length of the list).

NOTE *All the code under **define draw slice** could have been put in the other script's **forever** loop, but then it wouldn't have run in Turbo Mode. The Run without screen refresh option that you checked when you made the **draw slice** block enables Turbo Mode for the code in **define draw slice**. Otherwise, the slice drawing would be too slow for the game.*

SAVE POINT

Click the green flag to test the code so far. Hold down the mouse button and drag the cursor around the Stage. Make sure the light blue trail is drawn behind the mouse cursor and that it quickly disappears when the mouse button is released. Then click the red stop sign and save your program.

Ⓒ MAKE THE BEGIN BUTTON

Fruit Slicer requires the player to have quick reflexes. So let's add a button to the start screen to give the player a chance to get ready to play. Slicing a begin button with the mouse will start the game.

7. Create the Begin Button Sprite

You don't need to draw the begin button, because Scratch already has one. Click the **Choose sprite from library** button next to New sprite. Select **Button1** from the Sprite

Library window and click **OK**. Open the Info Area for this sprite and rename it Begin Button.

Click the **Costumes** tab at the top of the Blocks Area. Select the white color; then, using the Text tool, type *begin* and click somewhere on the canvas but not on the text. Then resize and drag the text over the bottom part of the green button.

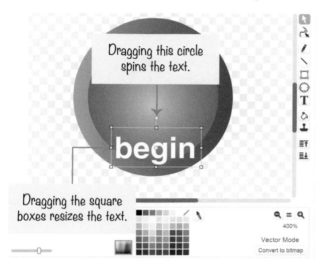

Using the Text tool, create the text *begin* again. And again, click somewhere on the canvas but not on the text. Grab the top handle of the text box and rotate the text so it's upside down. Then position it at the top of the green button.

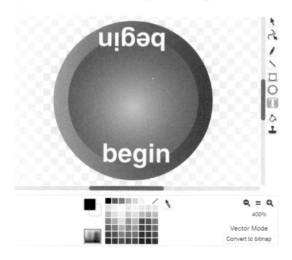

Add this code to the Begin Button sprite:

Set the color in the **touching color?** block to the color of the Slice sprite in the Sprite List. Click the block's color square, and then click the light blue color, as you did in Step 6.

The Begin Button slowly rotates on the Stage until the player slices it. The button knows it's been sliced when the light blue slicing color touches it, at which point it broadcasts the start game message to all the other sprites.

SAVE POINT

Click the green flag to test the code so far. Slice the Begin Button sprite. Make sure it disappears and the backdrop changes when it's sliced. Then click the red stop sign and save your program.

Ⓓ MAKE THE FRUIT AND BOMBS THROW THEMSELVES

Because the fruits in the game look different but have the same behavior, you'll use one sprite with the same code but different costumes.

8. Create the Fruit Sprite

Click the **Choose sprite from library** button next to New sprite, and select **Apple** from the Sprite Library. Then click **OK**. Click the new sprite's ⓘ button to open the Info Area, and rename the sprite Fruit.

Click the Fruit sprite's **Costumes** tab. Click the **Choose costume from library** button next to New costume. Add the banana costume. Click the button again and add the orange costume. Then click the button one more time to add the watermelon-a costume. Make sure the order of the costumes matches the following figure. If they're not in this order, drag the costumes into the correct order.

The Costume Library doesn't have a bomb costume, so you'll have to draw one for the Fruit sprite. If the player accidentally slices the bomb, they lose the game. In the Paint Editor, click the **Paint new costume** button next to New costume.

In the Paint Editor, draw a bomb with a red *X* on it. Use the Circle tool to draw the main body of the bomb and the Line tool to draw the top and *X*. Slide the Line width slider to make the lines thicker or narrower. Rename this costume bomb.

9. Make the Sliced Fruit Costumes

The Fruit sprite will have costumes for the four fruits, the bomb, and the sliced fruit. This step is easy because you don't have to draw anything. You'll just duplicate the costumes and pull them apart slightly so they look neatly sliced.

In the Paint Editor, right-click costume 1 (the apple costume) and select **duplicate** to create a second apple costume for costume 6.

Duplicate the banana, orange, watermelon-a, and bomb costumes as well. Make sure they're in the same order as the original costumes:

1. apple
2. bananas
3. orange
4. watermelon-a
5. bomb
6. apple2
7. bananas2
8. orange2
9. watermelon-a2
10. bomb2

NOTE *Double-check the order of the costumes! It can be hard to figure out how to fix the costume order later on. Being extra careful now can save you a lot of future frustration.*

For the code to work with every fruit, the sliced fruit's costume number will be five more than the unsliced costume. So the apple costume is costume 1, and the sliced apple is costume 6. The banana costume is costume 2, and the sliced banana is costume 7. This is the reason the order of the costumes is important. Also, you need a second bomb costume for costume 10. Duplicate the bomb costume, but you don't have to draw a sliced version of it.

The fruit costumes were drawn in Scratch's Vector Mode, which means they were drawn as a collection of shapes rather than as a grid of pixels. Although vector images look better than bitmap images, vector images can't be split in half with the Paint Editor's drawing tools. You'll need to convert the costumes to Bitmap Mode first.

For each duplicated fruit costume (costumes 6, 7, 8, and 9), select the costume and click the **Convert to bitmap** button in the lower right of the Paint Editor. Then use the Select tool to drag a selection rectangle over half of the costume. Drag the selected half away from the other half a bit, and rotate it a little to make it look like it's been cut in half.

You must be in Bitmap Mode to switch the costume.

You can also select and rotate the other half a little. Repeat this step for the duplicated bananas, orange, and watermelon-a costumes.

10. Add the Code to the Fruit Sprite

The Fruit sprite now has all the costumes it needs, so let's code its behavior. The Fruit sprite creates clones of itself, and each clone will randomly choose costume 1, 2, 3, 4, or 5. Then the clone throws itself up in the air. The clone will detect if it was sliced and switch to its sliced costume. Or, if the clone randomly chose the bomb costume and the player slices it, it will end the game.

Create For this sprite only variables named x velocity, y velocity, rotation speed, and number of fruit. All clones will use these variables to determine how they are thrown up and fall down. Make sure these variables are For this sprite only. The only For all sprites variables in this program are Score and High Score.

If the bomb is sliced, the game will make a noise. Click the **Sounds** tab and then click the **Choose sound from library** button under New sound. Select alien creak2 and click **OK**.

With the variables and sounds set up, you can now add the code so the original Fruit sprite can create multiple clones of itself every second. You'll add the code for the clones in Step 11.

Add the following code to the Fruit sprite.

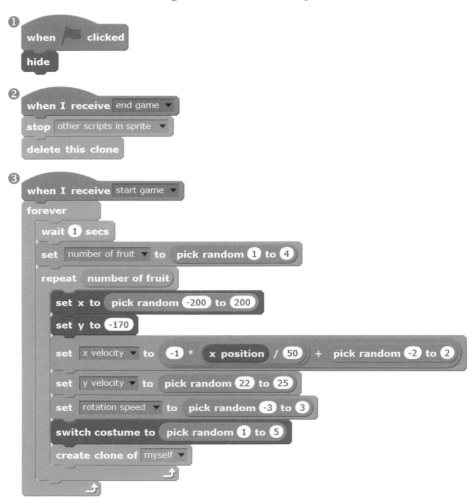

Script ❶ hides the fruit at the start of the game. Script ❷ cleans up the Stage when the game ends by deleting clones when the end game broadcast is received. Script ❸ runs when the player slices the Begin Button sprite and starts creating clones.

Let's take a closer look at how script ❸ works. After waiting 1 second, the number of fruit variable is set to 1, 2, 3, or 4. The code in the **repeat number of fruit** loop will create a new clone on each iteration. Inside the loop, the original Fruit sprite sets its x position to a random position and its y position to -170, placing the original Fruit sprite somewhere at the bottom of the Stage.

Next, the x velocity, y velocity, and rotation speed variables are randomly set (so the cloned fruit will be thrown randomly). The sprite's costume is also randomly set to costume 1, 2, 3, 4, or 5. All this code sets up the Fruit sprite to create a clone of itself. The clone's position, variables, and costume are cloned from the original Fruit sprite, which means the original is ready to randomly set itself up for the next clone.

The **set x velocity to** block uses a complicated equation, which is **-1 * x position / 50 + pick random -2 to 2**, for the x velocity variable's value. The x velocity value determines how far to the left or right the fruit is thrown. This should be a small value, so the sprite's **x position** (a random number from -200 to 200) is divided by 50, which is equal to a number between -4 and 4.

We always want the fruit to be thrown toward the center of the Stage. That means if the Fruit sprite is on the left side of the Stage, its x position will be negative and the clone should be thrown to the right. In other words, the x velocity variable should be set to a positive number. And if the Fruit is on the right (with a positive x position), it should be thrown to the left. This means the **x position / 50** number should be multiplied by -1; so if x position is positive, x velocity will be negative, and vice versa. Multiplying x velocity by -1 ensures that fruit on the left side of the Stage is thrown right and fruit on the right side is thrown left. Just to add some variation in the throws, a random number between -2 and 2 is added. You'll see how the clones use the x velocity variable in Step 11.

The x velocity and y velocity variables are used together so the fruit is thrown in a curved shape called a *parabola*. The mathematics of parabolas are used in many science and engineering applications, but you don't need to learn much about parabolas to use them in your games. Don't worry if you don't understand the math in these code blocks. As long as you copy the blocks from this book exactly as shown, your fruit will be thrown correctly.

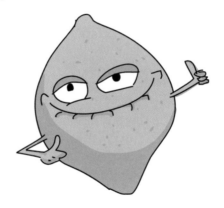

11. Add the Code for the Fruit Sprite's Clones

When the original Fruit sprite creates a clone of itself, the clone starts running its own code to throw itself up and detect if it's sliced.

First, create the missed fruit message by clicking the **broadcast** block's black triangle, selecting **new message**, and entering the name missed fruit. Then add the following code to the Fruit sprite.

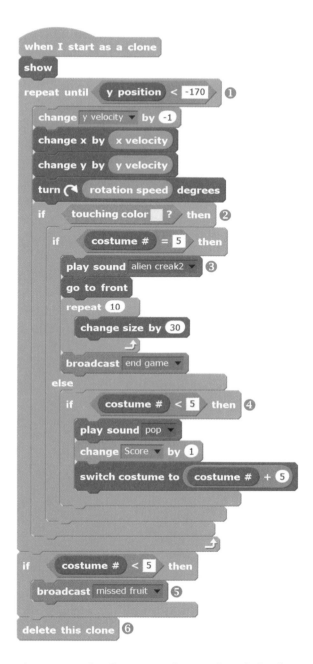

```
when I start as a clone
show
repeat until  ( y position  < -170 )  ❶
    change  y velocity ▼  by  -1
    change x by  ( x velocity )
    change y by  ( y velocity )
    turn ↻  ( rotation speed )  degrees
    if  < touching color ☐ ? >  then  ❷
        if  < costume #  = 5 >  then
            play sound  alien creak2 ▼   ❸
            go to front
            repeat 10
                change size by 30
            broadcast  end game ▼
        else
            if  < costume #  < 5 >  then  ❹
                play sound  pop ▼
                change  Score ▼  by 1
                switch costume to  ( costume #  + 5 )
    if  < costume #  < 5 >  then
        broadcast  missed fruit ▼   ❺
delete this clone  ❻
```

This script controls the Fruit clones, but it looks complicated, so let's break it down step-by-step. The original Fruit sprite is hidden, so the first thing the clone does is show itself.

Next, the code for gravity and slice detection repeats in a loop ❶ as long as the clone is up in the air. When the clone's y position drops below -170, the clone has fallen to the bottom of the Stage.

The first part of the **repeat until** block makes the clone fall faster under gravity by changing the y velocity by -1. Then the x position, y position, and direction of the clone are changed by the values in the x velocity, y velocity, and rotation speed variables, respectively, moving the fruit in a parabola-shaped path through the air. A parabola shape is drawn when the horizontal speed (in this case, x velocity) doesn't change but the vertical speed (in this case, y velocity) decreases over time.

The color in the **touching color** block should match the color of the Slice sprite ❷. The clone detects whether it has been sliced by checking whether it is touching the color of the Slice sprite's trail (see Step 6). If it is touching this color, the **if then else** block does another check for whether the costume number of the clone is set to 5 (which is the costume number of the bomb costume). If the bomb has been sliced, the Fruit clone makes the alien creak2 sound ❸, grows on the screen by running the **change size by 30** block, and then broadcasts the end game message.

Otherwise, if the sliced clone isn't set to costume 5 (that is, if it isn't the bomb costume), the code in the **else** part of the **if then else** block is run ❹. The **if then** blocks check which of the four fruit costumes the clone is set to, change the costume to the sliced form of that fruit, and add 1 to Score.

After the **repeat until y position < -170** block, if the costume is still set to one of the unsliced costumes (that is, costumes 1 to 4), the missed fruit message is broadcast ❺ (we'll take a look at the code that receives this message in Step 12). No matter if the costume is a sliced or unsliced fruit, the clone is then deleted ❻.

SAVE POINT

Click the green flag to test the code so far. Try slicing the fruit. Make sure the fruit changes to the sliced costume and the Score variable increases by 1. Then click the red stop sign and save your program.

 MAKE THE HEALTH SPRITES

The player doesn't want to slice all over the screen because they might hit a bomb. But to keep the player from being *too* cautious, you can end the game if the player misses three fruits.

12. Create the Health Sprite

The Health sprite will indicate how many more fruits the player can miss before losing the game. Each time the player misses a fruit, the sprite will switch to the next costume.

Click the **Paint new sprite** button next to New sprite. Open the Info Area for this new sprite and rename it Health. In the Paint Editor, use the Line tool to draw three blue *X*s and duplicate this costume three more times. I made my *X*s increase in size from left to right, but you can style yours any way you like as long as you have three of them.

Rename costume1 to 3 health, costume2 to 2 health, costume3 to 1 health, and costume4 to 0 health. Leave all three *X*s in 3 health blue. But for the other costumes, use the Fill tool, click the vertical gradient, and select a lighter red and a darker red color to paint the *X*s a red gradient. The costume 2 health will have one red *X*, 1 health will have two red *X*s, and 0 health will have three red *X*s. Make sure your costumes are in the same order as in the figure shown here:

The Health sprite will switch costumes based on different broadcast messages it receives. Add the following code to the Health sprite. All the messages should already exist by this step, so you shouldn't need to create them.

❶
```
when 🏳 clicked
hide
```

❷
```
when I receive start game ▾
switch costume to 3 health ▾
show
```

❸
```
when I receive missed fruit ▾
next costume
if  costume #  =  4  then
    broadcast end game ▾
```

❹
```
when I receive end game ▾
hide
```

When the player clicks the green flag and is at the start screen, the Health sprite hides itself in script ❶. When the player slices the Begin Button sprite, it broadcasts the start game message, and the Health sprite sets itself to show the 3 health costume in script ❷. Each time an unsliced fruit falls to the bottom of the Stage, that fruit broadcasts a missed fruit message, which makes the Health sprite switch to the next costume in script ❸. This next costume will have one more red X. If the Health sprite switches to 0 health, all three *X*s are red and the end game message is broadcast. When the Health sprite receives this message, it hides itself using the very short script ❹.

SAVE POINT

Click the green flag to test the code so far. Let some of the fruit fall without being sliced. Make sure the *X*s turn red for each missed fruit. Start a new game, and make sure the *X*s are all blue again. Then click the red stop sign and save your program.

ⓕ MAKE THE GAME'S ENDING

The player can lose in two different ways: when the player misses three fruits or when they slice a bomb. Either way, the end game message is broadcast, and several things happen as a result. The Fruit sprite's clones delete themselves, the Health sprite hides itself, and the Stage fades to white. We've already added code for the clones and the Health sprite, so let's add code that makes the Stage fade to white.

13. Create the White Fade Out Sprite

We'll use a ghost effect trick to make the Stage fade. Click the **Paint new sprite** button next to New sprite. In the Info Area, rename this sprite White Fade Out. In the Paint Editor, use the Fill tool to fill in the entire canvas with white. None of the white-gray checkered pattern on the canvas should be visible.

The White Fade Out sprite blocks most of the Stage. When the program begins, the White Fade Out sprite will hide itself and become visible only when the end game message is broadcast. Add the following code to the White Fade Out sprite:

When the White Fade Out sprite receives the end game message, it moves itself to the origin at the x- and y-coordinates (0, 0) ❶. Because the sprite is the same size as the Stage (480 pixels wide, 360 pixels tall), putting it at the origin makes it completely cover the Stage. The **go to front** block also places it in front of every other sprite. This makes sure that all the other sprites are behind it.

Before showing itself, the White Fade Out sprite sets its ghost effect to 100 ❷, making it completely invisible. Then the **repeat** loop decreases the ghost effect by 10 ten times ❸. The White Fade Out sprite gradually becomes more visible, and the white color slowly covers everything on the Stage.

If the Score variable is higher than the High Score variable, the High Score variable is updated ❹. After a short, 1 second delay, the White Fade Out sprite broadcasts the start screen message. The White Fade Out sprite hides itself, the Stage goes back to the start screen backdrop, and the Begin Button sprite shows itself ❺. The game looks like it did when the player clicked the green flag, but the High Score variable is set to the highest score achieved so far.

SAVE POINT

Click the green flag to test the code so far. Play the game and make sure that when you slice a bomb or when three fruits fall unsliced, the White Fade Out sprite fades into view and restarts the game. Then click the red stop sign and save your program.

The code for this program is too large to list the complete code in this book. You can view the completed code in the resources ZIP file—the filename is *fruitslicer.sb2*.

VERSION 2.0: HIGH SCORE

Scratch can store variables on its website using *cloud variables*. Scratch's cloud variables act just like regular variables except their value is remembered even after the web browser closes. Cloud variables are shared among every Scratcher using a program. You can make a competition for high scores using cloud variables for everyone who's played your game!

Because cloud variables use a lot of the Scratch website's bandwidth, there are some limitations for using them:

▸ Cloud variables store only numbers, not text.

▸ Cloud variables can't be used to make chat or multiplayer games.

▸ It takes a second or two for the cloud variable's value to update for everyone.

▸ New Scratchers who haven't used the website much can't use cloud variables.

The High Score variable shows the highest score a player has made. But using a cloud variable, you can make the game show the highest score of every player on the Scratch website! Select the White Fade Out sprite and click the **Make a Variable** button in the orange *Data* category. Enter the name Cloud High Score and make it a For all sprites variable (just like High Score). Then check the **Cloud variable (stored on server)** checkbox.

Check this box to make the variable a cloud variable.

NOTE   *If the Cloud variable checkbox isn't visible, it means you still have New Scratcher status and won't be able to use cloud variables until you've used the Scratch website more. Create more projects, talk on the discussion forums, and comment on other Scratcher's projects. Then wait a few days to see if your status has changed and the checkbox is available to you.*

When you've made the Cloud High Score variable, move its display on the Stage above the regular High Score variable.

Then add the following code to the White Fade Out sprite:

The **set Cloud High Score to Score** block changes the Cloud High Score variable for the player and also for every other player on the Scratch website. Now you have a high score system for all players ever!

CHEAT MODE: RECOVER HEALTH

You can add a secret button that will let a player recover lost health. This won't prevent the player from accidentally slicing bombs, but it can help them avoid losing health from dropping too many fruit. Pressing the R key will recover one health after you add the following code to the Health sprite. You can press the R key as often as you like during the game. Add the following code to the Health sprite.

if ⟨ costume # = **2** ⟩ then
  switch costume to 3 health ▼

if ⟨ costume # = **3** ⟩ then
  switch costume to 2 health ▼

SAVE POINT

Click the green flag to test the code so far. After dropping some fruit, press the R key and make sure that one health is recovered. You'll be able to see the red *X* turn blue. Then click the red stop sign and save your program.

SUMMARY

In this chapter, you built a game that

▶ Has a start screen instead of just beginning the game when the player clicks the green flag

▶ Uses gradients to draw backdrops and costumes

▶ Uses lists to track multiple values

▶ Tracks the position of the mouse with the **mouse x** and **mouse y** blocks

▶ Uses costumes to make clones of one sprite look like different kinds of fruit

▶ Returns to the start screen when the game ends instead of just stopping the program

▶ Remembers the high score of the player

This chapter was much longer than the previous chapters because the *Fruit Slicer* game is more sophisticated than previous games. But I think it's the most fun game in this book so far. As you continue to learn more about programming, you'll be able to make cooler games, so keep at it!

In Chapter 8, you'll create a space game where you shoot down incoming asteroids. Let's blast off!

REVIEW QUESTIONS

Try to answer the following practice questions to test what you've learned. You probably won't know all the answers off the top of your head, but you can explore the Scratch editor to figure out the answers. (The answers are also online at *http://www.nostarch.com/scratchplayground/*.)

1. In which code category can you create custom blocks?
2. What is the difference between the **call** and **define** blocks for a custom block?
3. What does the Run without screen refresh option do for custom blocks?
4. What does the **go to front** block do?
5. How is a list different from a variable?
6. How is a cloud variable different from a normal variable?
7. What does it mean when you don't see the Cloud variable (stored on server) checkbox?
8. Can cloud variables store text?
9. You see a sprite named Sprite1 in the Sprite List. How do you rename this sprite?

8

ASTEROID BREAKER . . . IN SPACE!

steroids is a classic game developed in 1979 by Atari. Since then, many programmers have remade the game, and it's a great programming project to make in Scratch, too. The player pilots a spaceship that must destroy space asteroids while avoiding the space pieces that break off . . . in space! (It's a well-known fact that adding " . . . in space!" makes everything more exciting.)

Instead of directly controlling where the spaceship moves, the player *pushes* the spaceship like a hockey puck on ice; because the player's ship has inertia, it slides around the Stage. To slow down the spaceship, players must push it in the opposite direction. It takes skill to move the spaceship without losing control, but that's half the fun of the game. The other half of the fun is blowing up asteroids.

Before you start coding, look at the final *Asteroid Breaker* program at *https://www.nostarch.com/scratchplayground/*.

SKETCH OUT THE DESIGN

Let's draw on paper what the game should look like. In our version of the game, the player controls their spaceship with the WASD keys and aims at incoming asteroids with the mouse.

Here is what my sketch looks like:

And here's what we'll be doing in each part:

A. Make a spaceship that is pushed around
B. Make the spaceship wrap around the edges
C. Aim with the mouse and fire with the spacebar
D. Make asteroids that float around
E. Make asteroids split in two when hit
F. Keep score and make a timer
G. Make the spaceship explode if it is hit

If you want to save time, you can start from the skeleton project file, named *asteroidbreaker-skeleton.sb2*, in the resources ZIP file. Go to *https://www.nostarch.com/scratchplayground/* and download the ZIP file to your computer by right-clicking the link and selecting **Save link as** or **Save target as**. Extract all the files from the ZIP file. The skeleton project file has all the sprites already loaded, so you'll only need to drag the code blocks into each sprite.

A. MAKE A SPACESHIP THAT IS PUSHED AROUND

Before we code the exciting parts of the game, we need to set up the backdrop and sprite. We'll make this game spacey by adding the stars backdrop and the spaceship sprite. Click the **Choose backdrop from library** button under New backdrop, select **stars**, and click **OK**.

We won't use the cat sprite that Scratch starts with, so right-click that sprite and select **delete** before continuing. Start a new project in the Scratch editor, and enter *Asteroid Breaker* as the project name.

1. Create the Spaceship Sprite

We'll use a flying saucer image for the spaceship, which you'll find in the resources ZIP file.

Click the **Upload sprite from file** button next to New sprite. Then select the *Spaceship.png* image file from the resources ZIP file.

In the orange *Data* category, click **Make a Variable** and create a variable named x velocity. Make x velocity a For this sprite only variable. Repeat the preceding steps to create a variable named y velocity.

NOTE   *If For this sprite only does not appear, the Stage is selected instead of the Spaceship sprite. Close the New Variable window, select the Spaceship sprite, and click **Make a Variable** again.*

You'll also need to create two variables named Score and player is alive, but make these variables For all sprites.

Next, add the following code to the Spaceship sprite. The code defines the ship's starting position and the initial values of variables; it also contains the logic that defines the user's controls.

```
when [flag] clicked
go to x: [0] y: [0]
show
set [player is alive ▼] to [yes]
set [Score ▼] to [10]
set [x velocity ▼] to [0]
set [y velocity ▼] to [0]
forever
    if < key [d ▼] pressed? > then
        change [x velocity ▼] by (0.5)
    if < key [a ▼] pressed? > then
        change [x velocity ▼] by (-0.5)
    if < key [w ▼] pressed? > then
        change [y velocity ▼] by (0.5)
    if < key [s ▼] pressed? > then
        change [y velocity ▼] by (-0.5)
    change x by (x velocity)
    change y by (y velocity)
```

You might be wondering why we didn't reuse code from previous games in which we used the **change x by** or **change y by** block. In this program, holding down one of the WASD keys adds to or subtracts from the x velocity and y velocity variables. Then the code at the bottom of the script changes the x and y position of the Spaceship sprite by using the values in these variables. Even after the player lets go of the key, the variables still reflect the updated position, so the spaceship continues to move.

Click the green flag to test the code so far. Press the WASD keys to see how the spaceship gets pushed. Make sure all four WASD keys push the spaceship in the correct directions. Then click the red stop sign and save your program.

B MAKE THE SPACESHIP WRAP AROUND THE EDGES

When you tested the code, did you notice that the Spaceship sprite stops immediately when it runs into the edge of the Stage? The reason is that Scratch prevents sprites from moving off the Stage, which is helpful in most Scratch programs. But in *Asteroid Breaker*, we want sprites to go off the side of the Stage and *wrap around* to the other side.

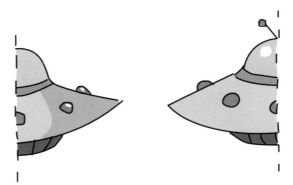

2. Add the Wrap-Around Code to the Spaceship Sprite

The following code will make the spaceship travel to the other side of the Stage whenever it reaches an edge. Add this code now.

```
when ⚑ clicked
forever
    if   x position < -235   then
        set x to 235
    if   x position > 235   then
        set x to -235
    if   y position < -175   then
        set y to 175
    if   y position > 175   then
        set y to -175
```

   The left and right edges of the Stage are at x-coordinates −240 and 240, respectively. The bottom and top edges of the Stage are at the y-coordinates −180 and 180. We use these boundaries to write code that changes the position of the Space-ship sprite when it goes past these four coordinates. Whenever the **x** or **y position** of the Spaceship sprite gets within 5 steps of these edges, this new code will move the Spaceship sprite to the other side of the Stage. Because the x velocity and y velocity variables will still be moving the Spaceship sprite at the same speed and in the same direction, the Spaceship sprite will look like it's moving continuously around the Stage.

SAVE POINT

Click the green flag to test the code so far. Make sure that all four edges send the Spaceship sprite to the other side. Then click the red stop sign and save your program.

3. Add the Random-Push Code to the Spaceship Sprite

The controls for this game offer a challenge, but let's make playing the game even more difficult. We'll add random little pushes to the Spaceship sprite so that the player can't just stay in the center without moving at all.

Add the following code to the Spaceship sprite to make random pushes happen every second:

```
when [flag] clicked
forever
    wait 1 secs
    change x velocity by pick random -1.5 to 1.5
    change y velocity by pick random -1.5 to 1.5
```

Inside the **forever** loop, the x velocity and y velocity variables are changed by a small, random amount after a 1 second pause. This means that every second the spaceship's movement receives a random push.

SAVE POINT

Click the green flag to test the code so far. Don't press any of the WASD keys. Wait to see if the spaceship starts moving a little on its own. Then click the red stop sign and save your program.

© AIM WITH THE MOUSE AND FIRE WITH THE SPACEBAR

The code that controls the Spaceship sprite is complete, so let's add energy blasts. These blasts will bust up those dangerous space asteroids! In space!

4. Create the Energy Blast Sprite

Scratch's Sprite Library has a sprite we can use for the energy blasts. Click the **Choose sprite from library** button next to New sprite. Select the Ball sprite and click **OK**. Open the sprite's Info Area by clicking the ❶ button, and rename it Energy Blast.

We want the Energy Blast sprite to make a laser sound when the Spaceship sprite fires it. Click the **Sounds** tab above the Blocks Area. Then click the **Choose sound from library** button under New sound. Select the laser1 sound and click **OK**.

We'll make clones of the Energy Blast sprite, but the clones and original sprite will run different code. There is only one Energy Blast sprite, but the player should be able to fire many energy blasts at once. We'll create clones of the original Energy Blast sprite so that more than one energy blast can be on the Stage. The original sprite will remain hidden; all the Energy Blast sprites that appear on the Stage will be clones.

We'll use a variable named I am a clone to keep track of which is the original sprite and which are clones. Click the **Scripts** tab to go back to the Scripts Area. In the orange *Data* category, click the **Make a Variable** button. Create a For this sprite only variable named I am a clone. The original Energy Blast sprite will set this variable to no, and the clones will set it to yes. Add the following code to the Energy Blast sprite:

The original sprite hides itself at the start of the game and remains hidden. The clones it makes will appear on the Stage. Also, the sprite we're using is too big for the game, so set its size to 10 percent to make it smaller.

Now add the following script to the Energy Blast sprite. The player will fire an energy blast by pressing the spacebar. The original Energy Blast sprite will create clones that show themselves and move toward the mouse. Since the Energy Blast clones move toward the mouse, the player can move the mouse to aim the energy blasts.

```
when space ▼ key pressed
if    player is alive  = yes  and   I am a clone  = no   then
    go to Spaceship ▼
    point towards mouse-pointer ▼
    create clone of myself ▼
```

The code under the **when space key pressed** block will run for the original sprite *and* the clones if we don't give instructions that this code should only run for the original sprite. But we don't want the existing clones to create new clones. The **if then** block checks that the I am a clone variable is set to no so that only the original Energy Blast sprite runs this code and creates clones.

Obviously, the Spaceship sprite can fire Energy Blast clones only if the player is alive, so the code also checks that the player is alive variable is set to yes.

Next, add the following code to the Energy Blast sprite so that the clones move toward the mouse after they've been created.

```
when I start as a clone
set  I am a clone ▼  to  yes
show
play sound  laser1 ▼
repeat  50
    move  10  steps
    if   ⟨ x position  <  -235 ⟩  then
        set x to  235

    if   ⟨ x position  >  235 ⟩  then
        set x to  -235

    if   ⟨ y position  <  -175 ⟩  then
        set y to  175

    if   ⟨ y position  >  175 ⟩  then
        set y to  -175

delete this clone
```

The clone starts by showing itself and moving forward. The clones should also wrap around the edges of the Stage just like the Spaceship sprite, so we use similar code to do that here.

Notice that the clones will set their own I am a clone variable to yes. This is so that the clones do not run the code in the **when space key pressed** script. The **if then** block in that script runs the code only if **I am a clone** is set to no.

The clones move forward 10 steps at a time 50 times. That means the Energy Blast clones have a limited range and won't keep moving forever. After the loop finishes repeating 50 times, the clone deletes itself and disappears from the Stage.

D MAKE ASTEROIDS THAT FLOAT AROUND

Now we need targets for the player to hit. The asteroids in this game float around until an Energy Blast clone hits them. They'll repeatedly break apart into two smaller asteroids until they're small enough to be vaporized.

5. Create the Asteroid Sprite

Add the new asteroid sprite by clicking the **Upload sprite from file** button and selecting the *asteroid.png* file. This file is in the resources ZIP file. Click the orange *Data* category, and then click the **Make a Variable** button. Create a For this sprite only variable named hits. Repeat these steps to make variables named x velocity, y velocity, and rotation. All are For this sprite only variables. In Step 6, we'll use the hits variable to keep track of how many times the asteroid has been hit and the size of the asteroid.

Let's write some code that makes the Asteroid sprite create new clones that appear on the Stage; each clone will have a random velocity and rotation. The result will be an unpredictable asteroid swarm . . . in space!

Add the following scripts to the Asteroid sprite.

```
when [clicked]
hide
set size to (100) %
set [hits ▾] to (0)
forever
  go to x: (-235) y: (pick random (-175) to (175))
  create clone of [myself ▾]
  wait (pick random (8) to (12)) secs
```

```
when I start as a clone
show
set [x velocity ▾] to (pick random (-3) to (3))
set [y velocity ▾] to (pick random (-3) to (3))
set [rotation ▾] to (pick random (-3) to (3))
forever
  turn ↻ (rotation) degrees
  change x by (x velocity)
  change y by (y velocity)
```

Like the Energy Blast sprite, the original Asteroid sprite will hide itself and generate clones. New clones are created every 8 to 12 seconds. When the clone is created, it shows itself, is assigned random velocities and rotations, and begins moving.

Also, like the Spaceship and Energy Blast sprites, the Asteroid sprites will wrap around the edges of the Stage. Add the following script to the Asteroid sprite.

```
when I start as a clone
forever
  if <(x position) < (-235)> then
    set x to (235)
  if <(x position) > (235)> then
    set x to (-235)
  if <(y position) < (-175)> then
    set y to (175)
  if <(y position) > (175)> then
    set y to (-175)
```

Click the green flag to test the code so far. Make sure the Asteroid sprite slowly moves and rotates and that it wraps around the edges of the Stage. Also, make sure that new clones appear every 8 to 12 seconds. Then click the red stop sign and save your program.

E   MAKE ASTEROIDS SPLIT IN TWO WHEN HIT

When an Energy Blast clone hits an Asteroid, the Asteroid will create two new smaller clones of itself, making it look like the Asteroid on the Stage split in two.

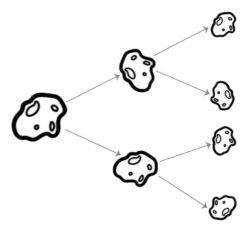

6. Add the Asteroid's Splitting Code

From the Sounds tab, click the **Choose sound from library** button. Then select chomp and click **OK**. The chomp sound will play whenever a clone hits the asteroid.

Add the following script to the Asteroid sprite. You'll need to create a new broadcast message named asteroid blasted.

When an Energy Blast clone hits an Asteroid clone, the Asteroid clone will play the chomp sound effect and broadcast the asteroid blasted message.

Then the Asteroid adds 2 points to the Score variable and increases the hits variable by 1. The hit Asteroid sprite will also shrink a little, changing its size by -25, so that when it (the "parent") clones itself twice, its "child" clones will be the smaller size. Finally, the Asteroid clone deletes itself.

The two smaller child clones will have hits variables that are one more than what the parent started with. The fourth time an Asteroid clone is hit, the hits variable is 4, and the code deletes the clone instead of creating two new clones. (The code after the **delete this clone** block doesn't run, because the clone no longer exists.) This prevents 1 Asteroid sprite from becoming 2, then 4, then 8, then 16, then 32, and exponentially more Asteroid sprites forever.

However, if you *do* want exponentially more Asteroid sprites, increase the number in the **if hits = 4 then** blocks.

7. Add the Asteroid Blasted Message Code to the Energy Blast Sprite

Select the Energy Blast sprite in the Sprite List, and add this script to it:

All the Energy Blast clones will receive the asteroid blasted message, but only those currently touching an Asteroid sprite will be deleted. (One will be touching an Asteroid, because the message is only broadcast by the Asteroid sprite when it is touching an Energy Blast sprite.) This is how an Energy Blast sprite disappears after hitting an Asteroid.

SAVE POINT

Click the green flag to test the code so far. Try blasting some of the asteroids. Make sure the energy blast disappears and the Asteroid sprite is replaced by two smaller clones. The fourth time an asteroid is hit, it should just disappear. Then click the red stop sign and save your program.

ⓕ KEEP SCORE AND MAKE A TIMER

The *Asteroid Breaker* game quickly becomes challenging when many tiny asteroids are flying around the Stage. A good game strategy is to be slow and careful, finishing off small Asteroid sprites before firing at larger ones. But we also want to put some pressure on the player, so let's make the Score variable start dropping by 1 point every second and have the game end when the Score is 0. This way, the player will have to keep up a quicker pace when blasting Asteroid sprites.

8. Create the Out of Time Sprite

Click the **Paint new sprite** button next to New sprite. In the Paint Editor, use the Text tool to write *OUT OF TIME* in red capital letters.

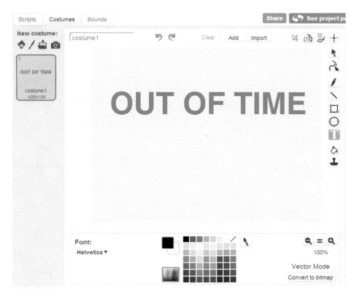

    Click this new sprite's ⓘ button in the Sprite List to open its Info Area. Rename the sprite Out of Time.

Add the following script to the Out of Time sprite.

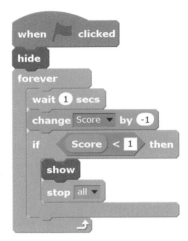

This code hides the Out of Time sprite at the start of the game and decreases the Score variable by 1 after a 1 second pause. When the Score variable reaches 0, the code shows the Out of Time sprite.

SAVE POINT

Click the green flag to test the code so far. Make sure the Score variable decreases by 1 point each second. When the Score variable is 0, the Out of Time sprite should display. Then click the red stop sign and save your program.

Ⓖ MAKE THE SPACESHIP EXPLODE IF IT IS HIT

A player can lose the game if they don't blast asteroids fast enough to prevent their Score from reaching 0. But they can also lose if an asteroid hits the spaceship. Let's add code to detect when this happens and display a cool explosion animation.

9. Upload the Explosion Sprite

Eight images are available for the frames of the explosion animation. These costumes are in the *Explosion.sprite2* file in the resources ZIP file.

In the Scratch editor, click the **Upload sprite from file** button next to New sprite. Select *Explosion.sprite2* and click **OK**. The eight costumes for the explosion animation appear on the sprite's Costumes tab.

10. Add the Code for the Explosion Sprite

For the Explosion sprite, you'll create a new broadcast message named explode. When the Explosion sprite receives this message, it will appear and switch through its costumes to display the explosion animation.

The Explosion sprite will also play a sound effect when the explosion happens. Load the sound by clicking the **Sounds** tab above the Blocks Area. Then click the **Choose sound from library** button under New sound. Select the alien creak2 sound and click **OK**.

Add the following code to the Explosion sprite:

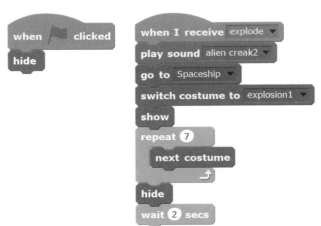

The Explosion sprite hides until it receives the explode broadcast. Then it plays a sound, goes to the position where the spaceship is, and switches its costumes seven times to create an awesome explosion animation!

11. Add the Explode Code to the Spaceship Sprite

The Spaceship sprite will broadcast the explode message when it touches one of the Asteroid clones. Add the following script to the Spaceship sprite:

The explosion animation works by briefly showing one of the costumes before moving to the next costume. This is similar to the frame-by-frame animation that cartoons and flipbooks use. Each costume is a frame, and the code quickly changes costumes to make the explosion look real.

SAVE POINT

Click the green flag to test the code so far. Make sure the Explosion sprite is not visible when the game starts. Fly into an asteroid, and make sure the Explosion sprite appears where the Spaceship sprite is. Then click the red stop sign and save your program.

The code for this program is too large to show here, but you can view the completed code in the resources ZIP file—the filename is *asteroidbreaker.sb2*.

VERSION 2.0: LIMITED AMMO

Once you get the hang of the game, *Asteroid Breaker* can become too easy. The one feature that makes it easy is that you can fire as fast as you can press the spacebar. This action lets the player fire indiscriminately instead of carefully aiming at the asteroids. But we can change that behavior by adding a new Energy variable. Firing an energy blast will reduce this variable by 1 each time. If the Energy variable is 0, the spaceship can't fire. The Energy variable will increase slowly over time, but it forces the player to carefully aim their shots and not waste them.

You'll need a variable to keep track of the spaceship's energy level. Select the orange *Data* category, and click the **Make a Variable** button. Make a variable named Energy, and select **For all sprites**. In the Blocks Area, make sure the checkbox next to Energy is checked (just like the checkbox for Score is checked) so that it will appear on the Stage.

The Energy variable will start at 10 at the beginning of the game and then decrease by 1 each time the player fires an energy blast. The player should be able to fire only if the Energy variable is larger than 0.

Modify the code in the Energy Blast sprite to match the following.

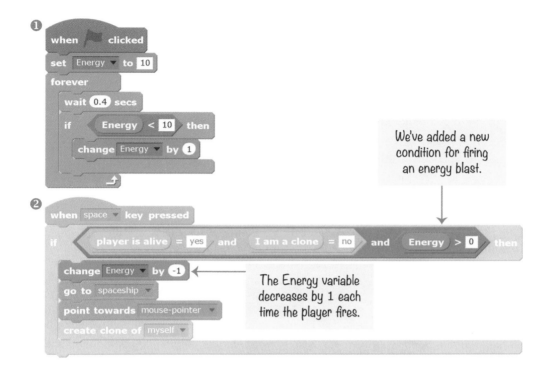

1

```
when [flag] clicked
set Energy to 10
forever
    wait 0.4 secs
    if  Energy < 10  then
        change Energy by 1
```

We've added a new condition for firing an energy blast.

2

```
when space key pressed
if  player is alive = yes  and  I am a clone = no  and  Energy > 0  then
    change Energy by -1
    go to spaceship
    point towards mouse-pointer
    create clone of myself
```

The Energy variable decreases by 1 each time the player fires.

Script **1** is brand new. It first sets the Energy variable to 10 before entering the **forever** loop. Inside the loop, if Energy is less than 10, it waits for 0.4 seconds before increasing Energy by 1. This way, the Energy value never goes above 10. Script **2** is slightly modified so that Energy must be greater than 0 in order for the player to fire. When an energy blast is fired, the **change Energy by -1** block decreases the Energy value.

SAVE POINT

Click the green flag to test the code so far. Make sure the Energy variable is visible on the Stage near the Score variable. The Energy variable should be 10 at the start of the game and decrease by 1 each time the player presses the spacebar. When the Energy variable is at 0, pressing the spacebar should not fire any more Energy Blast clones. Also, make sure the Energy variable recharges by 1 about every half second. Then click the red stop sign and save your program.

CHEAT MODE: STARBURST BOMB

The limited energy in *Asteroid Breaker* version 2.0 is more challenging, but let's add a secret cheat to work around it. A cheat to have unlimited energy would be boring, so instead we'll add a special energy bomb that fires in a starburst pattern all around the spaceship.

The starburst will fire when the player presses the X key. This code is similar to the regular firing code when the player presses the spacebar.

Add the following code to the Energy Blast sprite:

```
when x ▼ key pressed
if    player is alive = yes   and   I am a clone = no    then
    go to spaceship ▼
    point towards mouse-pointer ▼
    repeat 24
        create clone of myself ▼
        turn ↺ 15 degrees
```

Like the **when space key pressed** script, this script checks that the player is alive and that the sprite is not a clone. Only the original sprite should run this code, not the clones.

Inside the **if then** block, the Energy Blast sprite moves to the spaceship and points in the direction of the mouse. Then, the sprite clones itself 24 times. After each clone is made, the sprite changes direction by 15 degrees counterclockwise. This results in a starburst of energy blasts in all directions.

SAVE POINT

Click the green flag to test the code so far. Press the X key and watch Energy Blast clones fly out of the Spaceship sprite in all directions. Because this cheat move is a secret, make sure the player can use it no matter what the energy level is. Then click the red stop sign and save your program.

SUMMARY

In this chapter, you built a game that does the following:

▶ Uses a hockey-puck push style to control a spaceship

▶ Has x velocity and y velocity variables to keep track of how fast the Spaceship sprite is moving

▶ Lets sprites wrap around the edges of the Stage

▶ Has Asteroid clones that can create two smaller clones of themselves

▶ Has variables Score and Energy that constantly decrease and increase, respectively, over time

▶ Has frame-by-frame animation for an explosion

This game offers players a real challenge, but as programmers, we had to add those features one by one! The player doesn't directly control the spaceship but instead pushes it. If we stopped coding the Spaceship sprite at that point, the player could just hide in a corner, safe from asteroids, so we made all the sprites wrap around the edges. Even with that addition, the player might have tried to stay still in the center of the Stage. That's when we added random small pushes to the spaceship.

It's difficult to avoid many small asteroids, so the player could have taken it slow and carefully finished off small asteroids before targeting large ones. At that point, we made the score decrease over time to encourage the player to fire faster. The player could also keep blasting willy-nilly without aiming carefully, so we made an Energy variable to limit how fast the player could fire.

Each time you add a feature to your games, keep in mind how it affects gameplay. A game that is too hard to play is frustrating, but a game that is too easy is boring. It's all about finding a balance.

The next game is the most advanced program yet: it's a platformer game like *Super Mario Bros.* or *Super Meat Boy*. Not only will it have jumping and gravity like the *Basketball* game, but you'll be able to design custom levels for it without changing the code!

REVIEW QUESTIONS

Try to answer the following practice questions to test what you've learned. You probably won't know all the answers off the top of your head, but you can explore the Scratch editor to figure out the answers. (The answers are also online at *http://www.nostarch.com/scratchplayground/*.)

1. How does the wrap-around code work?
2. Why does the Energy Blast sprite have an I am a clone variable?
3. What prevents the Asteroid clone from breaking into exponentially more pieces forever?
4. How does the Explosion sprite's code make it look like the spaceship explodes?

9

MAKING AN ADVANCED PLATFORMER

The first *Super Mario Bros.* game was introduced in 1985 and became Nintendo's greatest video game franchise and one of the most influential games of all time. Because the game involves making a character run, jump, and hop from platform to platform, this game style is called a *platformer* (or *platform* game).

In the Scratch game in this chapter, the cat will play the part of Mario or Luigi. The player can make the cat jump around a single level to collect apples while avoiding the crabs who will steal them. The game is timed: the player has just 45 seconds to collect as many apples as possible while trying to avoid the crabs!

Before you start coding, look at the final program at *https://www.nostarch.com/scratchplayground/*.

Get ready to program a more complicated game than those in previous chapters!

SKETCH OUT THE DESIGN

Let's sketch out on paper what the game should look like. The player controls a cat that jumps around while apples appear randomly. The crabs walk and jump around the platforms randomly, too.

Here's what we'll do in each part:

A. Create gravity, falling, and landing
B. Handle steep slopes and walls
C. Make the cat jump high and low
D. Add ceiling detection
E. Use a hitbox for the cat sprite
F. Add a better walking animation
G. Create the level
H. Add crab enemies and apples

This platform game is the most ambitious one in the book, but anyone can code it if they follow the steps in this chapter. Let's code each part one step at a time.

If you want to save time, you can start from the skeleton project file, named *platformer-skeleton.sb2*, in the resources ZIP file. Go to *https://www.nostarch.com/scratchplayground/*

and download the ZIP file to your computer by right-clicking the link and selecting **Save link as** or **Save target as**. Extract all the files from the ZIP file. The skeleton project file has all the sprites already loaded, so you'll only need to drag the code blocks into each sprite.

(A) CREATE GRAVITY, FALLING, AND LANDING

In the first part, we'll add gravity, falling, and landing code, similar to the *Basketball* game in Chapter 4. The important difference is that in the platform game, the cat lands when it touches a ground sprite rather than the bottom of the Stage. Coding is a bit trickier, because we want the ground to have hills and eventually platforms!

To start, click the text field at the top left of the Scratch editor and rename the project from *Untitled* to *Platformer*.

1. Create the Ground Sprite

Let's use a simple shape for the ground in the first few scripts, just to explore how the code will work.

Click the **Paint new sprite** button next to New sprite to create a temporary ground sprite while you learn about platforming code. In the Paint Editor, use the Brush or Line tool to draw a shape for the ground. You can make the lines thicker by using the Line width slider in the bottom-left corner of the Paint Editor. Be sure to draw a gentle slope on the right and a steep slope on the left.

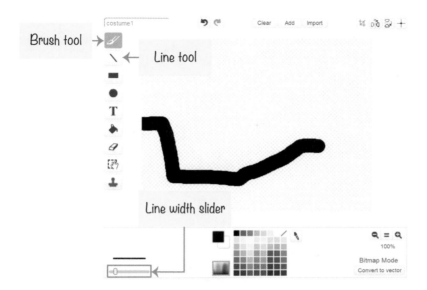

Brush tool →

Line tool

Line width slider

Open the sprite's Info Area and rename the sprite Ground. Also, rename the Sprite1 sprite Cat.

2. Add the Gravity and Landing Code

Now that we have a sprite for the ground, we need the cat to fall and land on it.

Select the Cat sprite. In the orange *Data* category, click the **Make a Variable** button and create a For this sprite only variable named y velocity. Then add the following code to the Cat sprite:

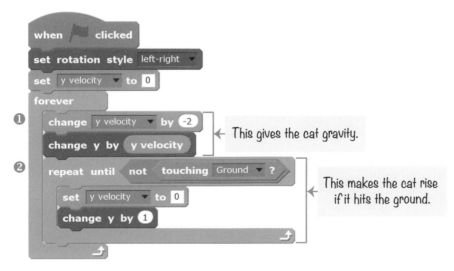

① ← This gives the cat gravity.

② ← This makes the cat rise if it hits the ground.

This code performs two actions in its **forever** loop: it makes the Cat sprite fall until it touches the Ground sprite ❶ and then lifts up the Cat sprite if it is deep in the ground ❷.

With these two code sections, the cat will fall down, hit the ground, and then rise if necessary, eventually settling on top of the Ground sprite.

In the air, falling down | Hitting the ground and rising up | Resting on top of the ground

The falling code at ❶ subtracts 2 from the y velocity variable and then moves the Cat sprite's y position by y velocity, making the cat fall faster and faster. If you programmed the *Basketball* game in Chapter 4, the falling code should be familiar.

But the **repeat until** block ❷ will loop until the Cat sprite is no longer touching the Ground sprite. (If the cat is still in the air and falling, it will not be touching the ground, so the code in the loop is skipped.) Inside this loop, the y velocity is set to 0 so that the Cat stops falling any farther. The **change y by 1** block will lift up the Cat sprite a little. The **repeat until not touching Ground** block continues lifting the sprite until it is no longer sunk into the Ground sprite. This is how the cat stays on top of the ground, no matter what the shape of the Ground sprite is.

SAVE POINT

Click the green flag to test the code so far. Drag the cat up with the mouse and let go. Make sure the cat falls and sinks into the ground a bit and then slowly lifts out of it. Then click the red stop sign and save your program.

3. Make the Cat Walk and Wrap Around the Stage

The cat also needs to walk left and right using the WASD keys, so add the following script to the Cat sprite:

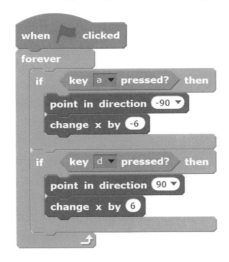

This code is very straightforward: pressing A points the cat to the left (-90) and moves the x position by -6 (to the left); pressing D makes the cat point to the right and moves the x position by 6 (to the right).

Next, add the following script to make the Cat sprite wrap around to the top if it falls to the bottom of the Stage.

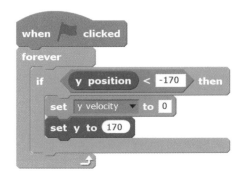

This code is very similar to the wrap-around code we wrote in the *Asteroid Breaker* game in Chapter 8. We'll write wrap-around code for moving left and right later.

SAVE POINT

Click the green flag to test the code so far. Press the A and D keys to make the cat walk up and down the slopes. If the Cat sprite walks off the edge of the Ground sprite and falls to the bottom of the Stage, the Cat sprite should reappear at the top. Then click the red stop sign and save your program.

This platformer has many scripts, so you might get lost if you get confused. If your program isn't working and you can't figure out why, load the project file *platformer1.sb2* from the resources ZIP file. Click **File ▶ Upload from your computer** in the Scratch editor to load the file, and continue reading from this point.

4. Remove the Ground Lift Delay

The big problem with the code right now is that the Cat sprite is lifted from inside the ground to on top of it very slowly. This code needs to run so fast that the player only sees the sprite on top of the ground, not in it.

The dark purple custom blocks can help us do this. Go to the *More Blocks* category, and click the **Make a Block** button.

Name the block **handle ground**, and then click the gray **Options** triangle. Check the checkbox next to **Run without screen refresh**.

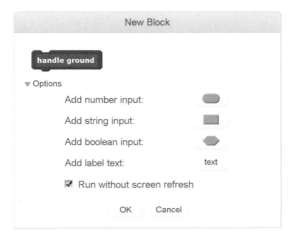

The **define handle ground** block should now appear in the Scripts Area. Change the code for the Cat sprite to make it use the **handle ground** block. The **handle ground** block goes where the **repeat until not touching Ground** blocks were, and that loop is moved under **define handle ground**.

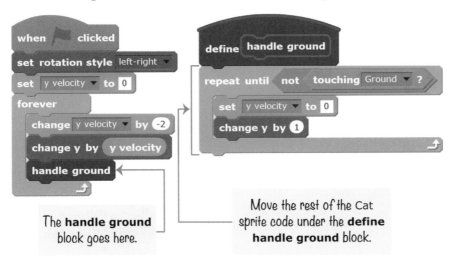

The **handle ground** block goes here.

Move the rest of the Cat sprite code under the **define handle ground** block.

This code works exactly as it did before, but now the **handle ground** block has Run without screen refresh checked, so the loop code runs in Turbo Mode. Lifting the cat now happens instantly, so it looks like the cat never sinks into the ground.

Click the green flag to test the code so far. Make the cat walk around or use the mouse to drop the cat from the top of the Stage as before. Now the Cat sprite should never sink into the ground. Then click the red stop sign and save your program.

If you're lost, open *platformer2.sb* in the resources ZIP file and continue reading from this point.

B HANDLE STEEP SLOPES AND WALLS

The Ground sprite has hills and slopes that the cat can walk on, and you can change the Ground sprite to pretty much any shape in the Paint Editor. This is a big improvement for the player compared to just walking on the bottom of the Stage, as in the *Basketball* game. But now the problem is that the Cat sprite can walk up the steep slope on the left as easily as it can walk up the gentle slope on the right. This isn't very realistic. We want the steep slope to block the cat. To do this, we'll make a small change to the walking code blocks.

At this point, the sprites are becoming overcrowded with lots of different scripts. So, right-click on the Scripts Area, and select **clean up** to reorganize the scripts into neat rows.

5. Add the Steep Slope Code

Now we need to edit the Cat sprite's walking code and add some new code, too. Instead of simply changing the x position by a particular value, we'll use a new custom block. Let's call it **walk** and give this new custom block an *input* called **steps**. An input is somewhat like a variable, but you can only use it in the custom block's **define** block.

Click the **Make a Block** button in the dark purple *More Blocks* category to make the **walk** block. Be sure to click the **Add a number input button** to make the **steps** input. When we want to call the new **walk** block, we'll have to define that input with a number of **steps** to take. Make sure you check the **Run without screen refresh** checkbox!

This code also requires you to make a variable for the Cat sprite named ground lift (which should be For this sprite only). We'll use this new variable to determine whether a slope is too steep for the cat to walk up. This code is a little complicated, but we'll walk through it step-by-step. For now, make the Cat sprite's code look like the following:

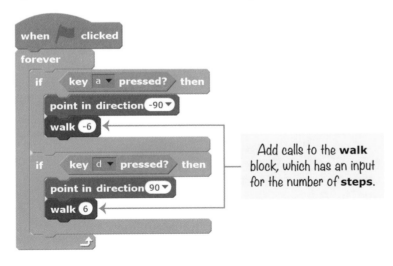

Add calls to the **walk** block, which has an input for the number of **steps**.

Add the new **walk** definition.

The value of **steps** is used to make the cat walk . . .

. . . and to prevent the cat from walking up steep slopes.

We want the cat to walk six units, as we did earlier, so we use -6 and 6 in the walking script when we call **walk**. In the **define walk** block, the **steps** input block is used in the **change x by** blocks. This makes the code more compact, because we can use the same script for moving the cat to the left (with the **walk -6** block) or to the right (with the **walk 6** block).

The code in the **repeat until** loop uses the ground lift variable to determine if the slope is a walkable slope or a wall that should block the Cat sprite's progress. The ground lift variable starts at 0 and changes by 1 each time the **repeat until** loop lifts the Cat sprite's y position by 1. This loop continues looping until the sprite is no longer touching the ground or ground lift is equal to 8.

If ground lift is less than 8, then the slope isn't that steep. The sprite can walk up the slope, so the **define walk** script doesn't have to do anything else.

But if **ground lift = 8**, the **repeat until** loop stops looping. This code means "the sprite has been lifted up by 8 but it's still touching the Ground sprite, so this must be a steep slope."

In that case, we need to undo the lift *and* the walking movement. The **change y by -8** and **change x by -1 * steps** blocks undo the Cat sprite's movement. Multiplying the **walk** input by -1 gives the opposite number of the input and variable.

Gentle slope: The Cat sprite is lifted eight steps and is no longer touching the ground. The Cat sprite can walk up this slope.

Steep slope: The Cat sprite is lifted eight steps but is still touching the ground. The Cat sprite cannot walk up this slope.

This code is exactly like the code in the *Maze Runner* game in Chapter 3 that blocks the player from walking through walls.

SAVE POINT

Click the green flag to test the code so far. Use the A and D keys to make the cat walk around. The cat should be able to walk up the gentle slope on the right, but the steep slope on the left should stop the cat. Click the red stop sign and save your program.

If you're lost, open *platformer3.sb* in the resources ZIP file and continue reading from this point.

◉ MAKE THE CAT JUMP HIGH AND LOW

With the walking code done, let's add jumping. In the *Basketball* game, we changed the falling variable to a positive number. This meant that the player jumped the height of that variable's value each time. But in many platform games, the player can do a short jump by pressing the jump button quickly or jump higher by holding down the jump button. We want to use high and low jumping in this platform game, so we'll have to come up with something a little more advanced than the *Basketball* game's jumping code.

6. Add the Jumping Code

Let's first create a For this sprite only variable named in air. This variable will be set to 0 whenever the Cat sprite is on the ground. But in air will start increasing when the Cat sprite is jumping or falling. The larger the in air value is, the longer the cat will have been off the ground and in the air.

Add this script to the Cat sprite:

```
when 🏳 clicked
forever
    if   key w ▼ pressed?  and   in air < 8   then
        set y velocity ▼ to 14
```

The **forever** loop keeps checking whether the W key is being held down. If it is, this will give the Cat sprite a velocity of 14—that is, the Cat sprite will be moving up. But note that there are two conditions for the cat to continue moving up—the player must hold down W *and* the in air variable must be less than 8.

Let's edit two of the existing Cat sprite scripts to add the in air variable that limits how high the cat can jump.

When the player first holds down the W key to make the cat jump, the y velocity variable is set to 14. This makes the code in the **forever** loop in script ❶ change the Cat sprite's y position by the positive y velocity, moving it upward. At the start of the jump, the in air variable is increasing but is still less than 8. So if the player continues to hold down the W key, y velocity keeps getting set to 14 instead of decreasing because of the **change y velocity by -2** block. This causes the jump to go upward longer than if the player had held down the W key for just one iteration through the loop. But eventually in air will become equal to or greater than 8, so it won't matter if the W key is pressed. Remember that both conditions—**key w pressed** *and* **in air < 8**—must be true for the code inside the **if then** block to run.

At this point, the y velocity variable will decrease as expected, and the Cat sprite will eventually fall. In script ❷, when the cat is on the ground, the in air variable is reset to 0.

D ADD CEILING DETECTION

The cat can walk on the ground, and now walls will stop the cat from moving through them. But if the player bumps the Cat sprite's head against a platform from below, the Cat sprite will rise above it! To solve this problem, we need to make some adjustments to the lifting code to add *ceiling detection*.

7. Add a Low Platform to the Ground Sprite

Add a short, low platform to the Ground sprite's costume, as shown in the following figure. Make sure it is high enough for the cat to walk under but low enough that the cat can jump up and touch it.

This platform should be low enough that the cat could hit its head on it. If it can't, then redraw the platform a little bit lower.

SAVE POINT

Click the green flag to test the code so far. Make the cat jump under the low platform. Notice that when the Cat sprite touches the platform, it ends up above the platform. This is the bug we need to fix. Click the red stop sign.

8. Add the Ceiling Detection Code

The problem with the code is in the custom **handle ground** block. This code always assumes the Cat sprite is falling from above, and if the Cat sprite is touching the Ground sprite, it should be lifted above it. The Ground sprite represents any solid part that the cat can't move through, including ceilings. We need to change the code so that if the Cat sprite is jumping up when it touches the Ground sprite, the cat *stops* rising because it bumps its head. We know the Cat sprite is moving upward when its y velocity is greater than 0. So let's edit the custom **handle ground** block to add a new Boolean input named **moving up**.

A *Boolean* is a true or false value. We use a Boolean input because we need to know if y velocity is greater than 0 when the **handle ground** block is first called. This true or false value is stored in the **moving up** input just like a variable would store it. If we put **y velocity > 0** in the **if then** block instead of **moving up**, then the cat would end up rising above the ceiling instead of bumping against it.

Right-click the **define handle ground** block and select **edit** from the menu.

Click the gray triangle next to **Options** to expand the window, and click the button next to **Add boolean input**. Name this new input field **moving up** and then click **OK**.

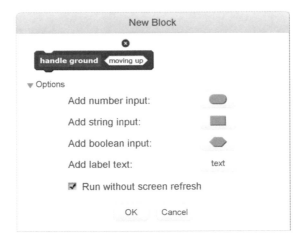

This will add a new **moving up** block that you can drag off the **define handle ground** block just like you do with blocks from the Blocks Area. This **moving up** block will be used in a new **if then else** block. Modify the **define handle ground** block's code to match this.

If the cat is moving up, the **change y by -1** block makes the cat look like it's bumping its head. Otherwise, the script behaves as it did previously, raising the cat so it sits above the ground.

Next, we have to edit the **handle ground** call in this script. We'll add a Boolean condition to determine whether the sprite is moving up, which is **y velocity > 0**.

The **handle ground y velocity > 0** block sets the **moving up** input to true if the y velocity is greater than 0 (that is, if the sprite is jumping and moving up). If y velocity is not greater than 0, then the sprite is either falling down or still, causing the **moving up** input to be set to false.

This is how the **define handle ground** block decides whether it should run **change y by -1** (so the Cat sprite can't go up through the ceiling) or run **change y by 1** (so the Cat sprite is lifted up out of the ground). Either way, if the Cat sprite is touching the Ground sprite (which it is if the code inside the **repeat until not touching Ground** block is running), the y velocity variable should be set to 0 so that the Cat sprite stops falling or jumping.

SAVE POINT

Click the green flag to test the code so far. Make the cat walk under the low platform and jump. Make sure the cat bumps into the platform but does not go above it. Then click the red stop sign and save your program.

If you're lost, open *platformer5.sb* in the resources ZIP file and continue reading from this point.

Ⓔ USE A HITBOX FOR THE CAT SPRITE

There's another problem with the game. Because the code relies on the Cat sprite touching the Ground sprite, any part of the Cat sprite can be "standing" on the ground, even its whiskers or cheek! In this figure, the cat isn't falling because its cheek has "landed" on the platform, which isn't very realistic.

Fortunately, we can fix this problem by using the hitbox concept we used in the *Basketball* game.

9. Add a Hitbox Costume to the Cat Sprite

Click the Cat sprite's **Costumes** tab. Then click the **Paint new costume** button and draw a black rectangle that covers most (but not all) of the area of the other two costumes. The following figure shows a slightly transparent first costume in the same image so you can see how much area the black rectangle covers.

Name this costume hitbox. Whenever the *Platformer* program's code checks whether the Cat sprite is touching the Ground sprite, we'll switch the costume to the black rectangle hitbox costume before the check and then back to the regular costume after the check. By doing so, the hitbox will determine whether the cat is touching the ground.

These costume switches will be handled with the dark purple custom blocks that have the option Run without screen refresh checked, so the hitbox costume will never be drawn on the screen.

10. Add the Hitbox Code

We'll add **switch costume to** blocks to the start and end of both dark purple custom blocks. Modify the Cat sprite's code to look like this:

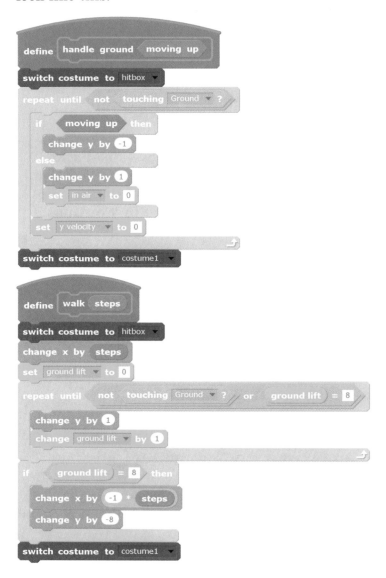

These blocks from the purple *Looks* category will change the costume to the hitbox. Because the hitbox is a simple rectangle that doesn't have protruding parts that could "catch" on platforms, like the cat's head and whiskers could, the game will behave in a more natural way.

SAVE POINT

Click the green flag to test the code so far. Make the cat jump around, and make sure the cat can't hang off the platform by its cheek or tail. Then click the red stop sign and save your program.

If you're lost, open *platformer6.sb* in the resources ZIP file and continue reading from this point.

F ADD A BETTER WALKING ANIMATION

The Cat sprite that a Scratch project starts with has two costumes named costume1 and costume2.

costume1   costume2

You can make a simple walking animation by switching back and forth between these two costumes. However, a Scratcher named griffpatch has created a series of walking costumes for the Scratch cat.

griffpatch has also made costumes for standing, jumping, and falling.

Using these costumes will make the *Platformer* game look more polished than using the two simple costumes that the Cat sprite comes with. We just need to add some animation code that switches between these costumes at the right time. griffpatch has created several cool Scratch programs using these costumes: *https://scratch.mit.edu/users/griffpatch/*.

11. Add the New Costumes to the Cat Sprite

To add the new costumes, you must upload the costume files into your Scratch project. You'll find the eight walking images and the standing, jumping, and falling images in the resources ZIP file. The filenames for these images are *Walk1.svg*, *Walk2 .svg*, and so on up to *Walk8.svg*, as well as *Stand.svg*, *Jump.svg*, and *Fall.svg*.

Then, in the Scratch editor, click the Cat sprite's **Costumes** tab. Click the **Upload costume from file** button next to New sprite, and select *Stand.svg* to upload the file. This creates a new sprite with *Stand.svg* as its costume.

Delete the original costume1 and costume2 costumes, but keep the hitbox costume. Put the costumes in the following order (it's important that you match this order exactly):

1. Stand
2. Jump
3. Fall
4. Walk1
5. Walk2
6. Walk3
7. Walk4
8. Walk5
9. Walk6
10. Walk7
11. Walk8
12. hitbox

Each costume has not only a name (like Walk1, Jump, or Fall) but also a number. The costume number is based on the costume's order in the Costumes tab. For example, the costume at the top is named Stand, but it is also known as costume 1. The costume beneath it is named Jump, but it is also known as costume 2. The code we add in the next step will refer to costumes by their names and numbers.

12. Create the Set Correct Costume Block

With all these different costumes, it will be a bit tricky to determine which frame we need to show and when. We'll use the idea of animation frames: several frames shown together quickly make a moving image, just like a flip book.

To keep track of the frames, create two For this sprite only variables named frame and frames per costume. Then add two **set** blocks for these initial variables to the Cat sprite's **when green flag clicked** script.

```
when ⚑ clicked
set size to 30 %
set rotation style left-right ▾
set y velocity ▾ to 0
set frame ▾ to 0
set frames per costume ▾ to 4
forever
    change y velocity ▾ by -2
    change y by y velocity
    change in air ▾ by 1
    handle ground < y velocity > 0 >
```

Now the setup is done.

As the player moves the Cat sprite left or right, we want the frame variable to increase. The frames per costume variable keeps track of how fast or slow the animation runs.

Let's edit the code in the **define walk** custom block to increase the frame variable by an amount calculated from frames per costume.

```
define walk steps
switch costume to hitbox ▾
change x by steps
set ground lift ▾ to 0
repeat until < not < touching Ground ▾ ? > or < ground lift = 8 >
    change y by 1
    change ground lift ▾ by 1
if < ground lift = 8 > then
    change x by -1 * steps
    change y by -1 * ground lift
change frame ▾ by 1 / frames per costume
```

When the cat is standing still (that is, not moving left or right), the frame variable should be reset to 0. Modify the Cat sprite's existing **when green flag clicked** script to add a third **if then** block that resets the frame variable.

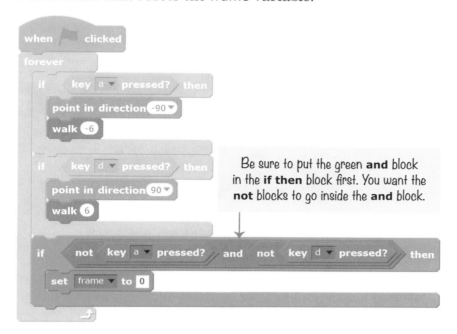

Be sure to put the green **and** block in the **if then** block first. You want the **not** blocks to go inside the **and** block.

Now let's write some code to determine which costume to show. We'll use this code in a few places in the scripts we've written, so let's make a custom block.

In the dark purple *More Blocks* category, click the **Make a Block** button and name this block **set correct costume**. Click the gray **Options** triangle, check the option **Run without screen refresh**, and then click **OK**. Add the following blocks to the Cat sprite, starting with the new **define set correct costume** block.

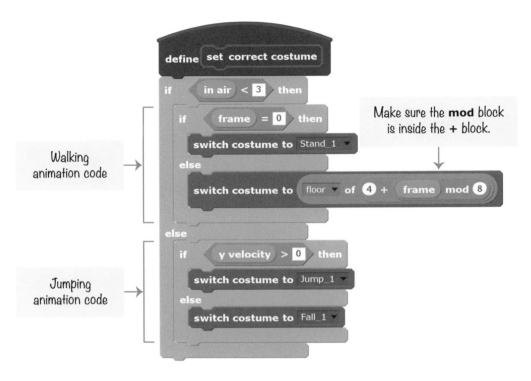

Walking animation code →

Jumping animation code →

Make sure the **mod** block is inside the **+** block.

If the Cat sprite is on the ground (or has just started jumping or falling so that in air is less than 3), then we want to display either the standing costume or one of the walking costumes. Remember that the **when green flag clicked** script keeps setting frame to 0 if the player isn't pressing the A key or D key. So when frame is 0, the **switch costume to Stand** block displays the Stand costume. Otherwise, we must calculate which of the eight walking costumes to show. This calculation refers to costumes by their numbers, which are based on their order in the Costumes tab.

Which walking costume is shown is decided by the **switch costume to floor of 4 + frame mod 8** blocks. Wow, that looks complicated! Let's break it down to better understand each part.

The **mod** block does a *modulo* mathematical operation, which is the remainder part of division. For example, 7 / 3 = 2 remainder 1, so 7 mod 3 = 1 (the remainder part). We'll use **mod** to calculate which costume number to display.

The frame variable keeps increasing, even though we only have eight walking costumes. When frame is set to a number from 0 to 7, we want it to display costumes 4 to 11. This is why our code has the **4 + frame** blocks. But when frame increases to 8, we want to go back to costume 4, not costume 12.

The **mod** block helps us do this wrap around with the costume numbers. We can control the costume that is displayed by using a math trick: because 8 mod 8 = 0, a frame value of 8 will show the first walking costume! We have to add 4 to this number, because the first walking costume is actually costume 4. (Remember, costume 1, costume 2, and costume 3 are the standing, jumping, and falling costumes, respectively.) This sum is then used with the **floor** block. *Floor* is a programming term that means "round down." Sometimes **frame** will be set to a number like 4.25 or 4.5, and so **4 + frame** would be 8.25 or 8.5, but we just want to round down to show costume 8.

Whew! That's the most math you've seen in this book so far, but when it's broken down, it becomes easier to understand.

The code in the **else** part of the **if then else** block handles what happens if in air is greater than or equal to 3. We check y velocity to see if the cat is falling (that is, if y velocity is less than or equal to 0) or jumping (that is, if y velocity is greater than 0) and switch to the correct costume. Finally, the **define set correct costume** code finishes.

Replace the **switch costume to costume1** blocks in the **define handle ground** and **define walk** blocks with the new **set correct costume** blocks. Also, add the **change frame by 1 / frames per costume** blocks so that the frame variable increases over time, as shown here.

```
define handle ground (moving up)
switch costume to [hitbox ▼]
repeat until <not <touching [Ground ▼]?>>
    if <(moving up)> then
        change y by (-1)
    else
        change y by (1)
        set [in air ▼] to (0)
    set [y velocity ▼] to (0)
set correct costume
```

```
define walk (steps)
switch costume to [hitbox ▼]
change x by (steps)
set [ground lift ▼] to (0)
repeat until <<not <touching [Ground ▼]?>> or <(ground lift) = (8)>>
    change y by (1)
    change [ground lift ▼] by (1)
if <(ground lift) = (8)> then
    change x by ((-1) * (steps))
    change y by (-8)
change [frame ▼] by ((1) / (frames per costume))
set correct costume
```

Click the green flag to test the code so far. Move the cat around the Stage, and make sure the walking animation displays correctly. Also, make sure the standing, jumping, and falling costumes are shown at the right times. Then click the red stop sign and save your program.

If you're lost, open *platformer7.sb* in the resources ZIP file and continue reading from this point.

G CREATE THE LEVEL

The new walking animation makes the *Platformer* game look more appealing. Now let's change the plain white background into a real level. What's great about the code we've written for the Cat sprite to walk, jump, and fall is that it will work with a Ground sprite of any shape or color. So if we change the Ground sprite's costume (say, for different levels) we don't have to reprogram the Cat sprite!

13. Download and Add the Stage Backdrop

Click the Ground sprite's **Costumes** tab. Click the **Upload costume from file** button and select *PlatformerBackdrop .png*, which is in the resources ZIP file. After this costume has uploaded, you can delete the previous costume.

It's not enough to add the file *PlatformerBackdrop.png* as a costume for the Ground sprite. You must also upload it as a Stage backdrop. Click the **Upload backdrop from file** button next to New backdrop, and select *PlatformerBackdrop.png* to upload it. We need to upload the file to both places because we'll be erasing all the "background parts" from the Ground sprite in the next step. We only need the Ground sprite to mark which parts the Cat sprite can walk on. The backdrop will be the image that is displayed on the Stage.

14. Create a Hitbox Costume for the Ground Sprite

The *Platformer* game code is based on the Cat sprite touching the Ground sprite. The Ground sprite's costume is a hitbox, so if the Ground sprite's costume is a full rectangle that takes up the entire Stage, it will be treated as though the entire Stage is solid ground. We need to remove the parts of the Ground sprite's costume that are part of the background and not platforms.

The easiest way to do this is to click the Select tool in the Paint Editor. Drag a Select rectangle over the part of the costume you want to delete. After selecting an area, press DELETE to remove that piece.

1. Click the Select tool.

2. Drag the Select rectangle over the area you want to remove and press DELETE.

Use the Eraser tool to erase areas that aren't rectangular. If you make a mistake, click the Undo button at the top of the Paint Editor to undo the deletion.

Keep removing the background parts of the costume until only the platform parts remain.

If you're having trouble creating this costume, you can use the premade *PlatformerBackdropHitbox.png* image in the resources ZIP file. The background parts of the image are already deleted, so you just need to click the **Upload costume from file** button on the Costumes tab to add it.

15. Add the Ground Sprite's Code

The Stage backdrop is used to set the appearance of the platforms and background. The Ground sprite is used to identify which parts are solid ground that the Cat sprite can walk on. Add the following code to the Ground sprite's Scripts Area:

The Ground sprite's costume needs to line up perfectly over the Stage's backdrop so that you can't tell it's there. Because the Stage backdrop and the Ground sprite's costume came from the same image file, you can do this by moving the Ground sprite to the coordinates (0, 0). Otherwise, the Ground sprite's costume won't line up perfectly over the backdrop.

The *drawing* of the Ground sprite's costume doesn't matter as much as the *shape* of the costume. As long as the Ground sprite is lying perfectly on top of the backdrop, we can set the ghost effect to 100, and the Ground costume and backdrop will line up. The backdrop shows what the level looks like, while the Ground sprite acts as its hitbox.

SAVE POINT

Click the green flag to test the code so far. Make sure you can move the cat all around the Stage. Then click the red stop sign and save your program.

16. Add More Wrap-Around Code to the Cat Sprite

Notice that the level has a couple floating platforms and a hill with a pit in the middle. When the cat falls down the pit, it wraps around the Stage and reappears at the top. Let's add wrap-around code for the left and right edges of the Stage as well. Add the following script to the Cat sprite.

```
when [flag] clicked
forever
    if < x position < -230 > then
        set x to 230
        if < y position < 5 > then
            set y to 5
    else
        if < x position > 230 > then
            set x to -230
```

When the cat walks to the left edge of the Stage, its **x position** will be less than -230. In that case, we make it wrap around to the right edge by setting the **x position** to 230.

Also, if the cat is moving from the left side of the Stage, its **y position** will be less than 5. This will put it inside the ground when moved to the right edge of the Stage, so an **if then** block checks for this condition and sets the **y position** to 5.

When you set the **y position** to 5, the cat ends up above the ground.

The cat wraps around the Stage.

If you don't change the **y position**, the cat ends up inside the ground.

The other **if then** block wraps the Cat to the left edge of the Stage if it's on the right edge (that is, its **x position** is greater than 230.)

SAVE POINT

Click the green flag to test the code so far. Make sure the cat can walk off the left edge of the Stage and wrap around to the right, and vice versa. Then click the red stop sign and save your program.

If you're lost, open *platformer8.sb* in the resources ZIP file and continue reading from this point.

Ⓗ ADD CRAB ENEMIES AND APPLES

The entire *Platformer* game setup is complete! The player can make the Cat sprite walk, jump, fall, and stand on platforms.

The Cat sprite has some cool animations, and the backdrop looks like a real video game.

Now all we have to do is make a game using all the pieces we have. We'll add an apple that appears randomly around the Stage (similar to the *Snaaaaaake* game in Chapter 6) and add a few enemies that try to touch the Cat sprite and steal the apples.

17. Add the Apple Sprite and Code

Click the **Choose sprite from library** button and select the Apple sprite from the Sprite Library window that appears; then click **OK**.

As in previous games, we'll use a variable to track the game's score. Click the orange *Data* category, and then click the **Make a Variable** button to create a For all sprites variable named Apples Collected. This variable will keep track of the player's score.

In the Apple sprite's Scripts Area, add the following code.

At the start of the game, when the player clicks the green flag, the score in Apples Collected is set to 0. Also, because the Apple sprite is a bit too big, we set its size to 50 percent.

During the game, the Apple sprite needs to appear in random places on the Stage. We make the Apple sprite invisible using **set ghost effect to 100**. It then moves to a random place on the Stage.

But not just any random place on the Stage will do. We need to make sure the Apple sprite is not inside the Ground sprite, because it would be impossible for the player to get it. To prevent the Apple sprite from moving to somewhere inside the Ground sprite, the loop keeps trying new random places until the Apple sprite is no longer touching the Ground sprite. The movement of the apple won't be visible to the player, because the ghost effect is still set to 100. When the Apple sprite finds a place that is not touching the Ground sprite, it becomes visible again with **set ghost effect to 0**.

Then the Apple sprite waits until the Cat sprite touches it. When that happens, the score in Apples Collected increases by 1, and the Apple sprite loops to find a new random place on the Stage.

SAVE POINT

Click the green flag to test the code so far. Make sure the Apple sprite never appears inside the ground. When the cat touches the apple, the score in Apples Collected should increase by 1, and the Apple sprite should move to a new random place. Click the red stop sign and save your program.

18. Create the Crab Sprite

The game wouldn't be very challenging if all the player had to do was jump around and collect apples. Let's add some enemies that the player must avoid.

Right-click the Cat sprite and select **duplicate**. The enemies will use the same code as the Cat sprite so that they can jump and fall on the platforms. (We'll remove the code that assigns the keyboard keys to control the sprite and replace it with code that moves the crabs around randomly.) Rename this duplicated sprite Crab. Then, in the Costumes tab, click the **Choose costume from library** button, select the crab-a costume, and click **OK**. Then open the Costume Library again and select the crab-b costume.

The Crab sprite will still have all the Cat sprite costumes (Stand, Fall, Walk1, and so on). Delete these Cat sprite costumes, including the hitbox costume. Create a new hitbox costume that is the right size for the crab. Here's what the hitbox costume should look like (the crab-a costume has been placed over it so you can see the relative size, but the costume is just the black rectangle).

19. Create the Enemy Artificial Intelligence

In games, *artificial intelligence (AI)* refers to the code that controls the enemies' movements and how they react to the player. In the platform game, the AI for the crabs is actually pretty *un*intelligent: the crabs will just move around randomly.

In the orange *Data* category, click the **Make a Variable** button and create a For this sprite only variable named movement. The movement variable will store a number representing the Crab sprite's movements:

1. Walk left
2. Walk right

3. Jump up straight
4. Jump to the left
5. Jump to the right
6. Stay still

The Crab sprite's movements will be randomly decided and will frequently change. Add the following code to the Crab sprite.

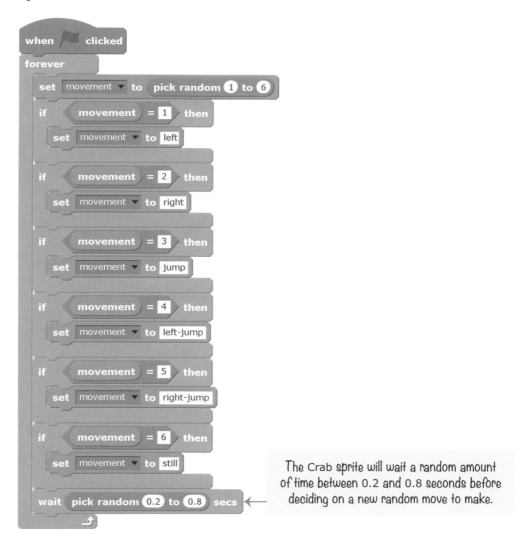

The Crab sprite will wait a random amount of time between 0.2 and 0.8 seconds before deciding on a new random move to make.

At first, the movement variable is set to a random number between 1 and 6 that decides which movement the crab will make.

The rest of the Crab sprite's code defines these movements. Find any code from the Cat sprite code that used the **when key pressed** blocks and replace those blocks with blocks that check the movement variable. (If you ran the program right now, the keyboard keys would control the Cat *and* Crab sprites, because they have the same code!)

Modify the Crab sprite script that checks whether the player is pressing the A key or D key to match the following code.

```
when [flag] clicked
forever
    if < movement = [left] or movement = [left-jump] > then
        point in direction (-90 ▼)
        walk (-4)
    if < movement = [right] or movement = [right-jump] > then
        point in direction (90 ▼)
        walk (4)
    if < movement = [still] > then
        set [frame ▼] to [0]
```

As with the Cat sprite, this code lets the Crab sprite walk left and right. Change the values in the **walk** blocks to -4 and 4 to make the crab move slower than the player.

Then change the script that handles the player pressing the W key to jump to match the following code.

This code lets the Crab sprite jump up, left, and right.

Now let's animate the crab's movements. The Crab sprite has only two costumes, crab-a and crab-b. We'll switch between these two costumes to make it look like the crab is walking. We can simplify the **set correct costume** block for the Crab sprite a bit.

Modify the **set correct costume** code to look like the following:

Notice that the numbers in the **floor of 1 + frame mod 2** blocks have also changed. The first costume is costume 1, and the Crab has only two costumes, so the numbers in these blocks have been changed to 1 and 2.

Finally, we need to create a new script so that the crabs can steal apples from the player. Add this code to the Crab sprite.

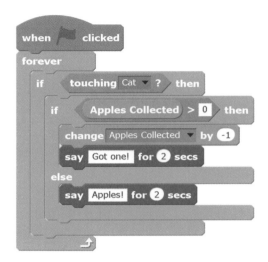

The Crab sprites subtract 1 from Apples Collected and say "Got one!" when they touch the player. If the player has 0 apples, the Crab sprites will say "Apples!" but will not subtract 1 from Apples Collected.

The game will be a bit more exciting with two crabs, so right-click the Crab sprite in the Sprite List and select **duplicate** from the menu.

SAVE POINT

Click the green flag to test the code so far. Make sure the two crabs are jumping around. When they touch the cat, they should steal an apple and say "Got one!" If the cat doesn't have any apples, the crabs should just say "Apples!" Then click the red stop sign and save your program.

20. Add the Time's Up Sprite

We're almost done! The last thing we need to add to the game is a timer. The player will be under pressure to grab apples as quickly as possible instead of playing it safe. Click the **Paint new sprite** button, and draw the text *Time's Up* in the Paint Editor. Mine looks like this:

Rename the sprite Time's Up. Then create a For all sprites variable named Timer, and add the following code.

This code gives the player 45 seconds to collect as many apples as possible while trying to avoid the crabs who will steal one. When the Timer variable reaches 0, the Time's Up sprite will appear and the game will end.

Now the *Platformer* game is ready for final testing!

Click the green flag to test the code so far. Walk and jump around, collecting apples while trying to avoid the crabs. Make sure that when the timer reaches 0, the game ends. Then click the red stop sign and save your program.

The code for this program is too large to list the complete code in this book. However, you can view the completed code in the resources ZIP file—the filename is *platformer.sb2*.

SUMMARY

You did it! You're a Scratch master! The advanced *Platformer* game is the most elaborate and complex project in this book. You combined and used lots of different concepts to make this game, so it might help to read through this chapter a few more times.

In this chapter, you built a game that

▶ Uses a ground sprite that the player stands on

▶ Uses dark purple custom blocks with the Run without screen refresh option enabled

▶ Lets the player walk up and down slopes

▶ Has ceiling detection so the player bumps their head on low platforms

▶ Has detailed animations for walking, jumping, and falling

▶ Implements AI for enemies so they move around on their own

That wraps it up for this book, but don't let that stop you from continuing your programming adventure. You can always look through other Scratcher's programs to get more ideas. Find a game you like, and try to create it from *scratch*. (All my puns are intended.)

The great thing about Scratch is that it provides you with unlimited possibilities for the types of games you can make. You can create clones of popular classic games like *Pac-Man* or *Flappy Bird*. Or you can make unique games using your own designs. Good luck!

REVIEW QUESTIONS

Try to answer the following practice questions to test what you've learned. You probably won't know all the answers off the top of your head, but you can explore the Scratch editor to figure out the answers. (The answers are also online at *http://www.nostarch.com/scratchplayground/*.)

1. The dark purple custom blocks help you avoid duplicating code. Why is this a good thing?
2. How is a dark purple custom block's input like a variable?
3. Where can you use a dark purple custom block's input?
4. What does *modulo* mean in mathematics?
5. What does *floor* mean in programming?

WHERE TO GO FROM HERE

Ready for more? There are plenty of Scratch resources to keep things exciting.

- **Scratch Programming Playground Studio** (*http://www.inventwithscratch.com/studio/*) is a place to share your own games based on the ones in the book! You can check out other readers' projects while you're there.

- **The Scratch Forums** (*http://scratch.mit.edu/discuss/*) is a place for Scratchers to share ideas and ask and answer questions.

- **Learn to Program with Scratch** by Majed Marji (No Starch Press, 2014; *https://www.nostarch.com/learnscratch/*), is a book with more projects for learning computer science concepts in Scratch.

- **ScratchEd** (*http://scratched.gse.harvard.edu/*), is an online community created for teachers and other educators who use Scratch. Share your success stories, exchange Scratch resources, ask questions, and more.

There are many fun games and animations you can make with Scratch, but it does have some limitations. Your Scratch programs might not look like "real" games you play on a PC, game console, or smartphone.

So it's only natural that you might want to learn how to write code in a professional programming language. There are many languages to choose from, but I recommend Python or JavaScript. Python is the easiest language to learn (aside from Scratch) but it is still a language used by professional software developers. JavaScript is not quite as easy, but it's the language used for web apps that run in your browser.

If you want to learn Python, I recommend a book I wrote: *Invent Your Own Computer Games with Python*. This book is free to read online at *https://inventwithpython.com/*, or you can buy it at *https://www.nostarch.com/inventwithpython/*. If you want to learn JavaScript, I recommend Nick Morgan's *JavaScript for Kids* (No Starch Press, 2014; *https://www.nostarch.com/javascriptforkids/*). These books are great for the next step of your journey to become a master programmer!

INDEX

RESOURCES

Visit *https://www.nostarch.com/scratchplayground/* for resources, errata, and more information.

MORE SMART BOOKS FOR CURIOUS KIDS!

INVENT YOUR OWN COMPUTER GAMES WITH PYTHON

by AL SWEIGART
DECEMBER 2016, 378 PP., $29.95
ISBN 978-1-59327-795-6

AUTOMATE THE MINECRAFT STUFF

Mine, Farm, and Build with Code

by AL SWEIGART
SPRING 2018, 260 PP., $29.95
ISBN 978-1-59327-853-3
full color

MAKE YOUR OWN VIDEO GAMES!

With PuzzleScript, Scratch, and Twine

by ANNA ANTHROPY
SPRING 2018, 340 PP., $24.95
ISBN 978-1-59327-794-9
full color

SCRATCH CODING CARDS

Creative Coding Activities for Kids

by NATALIE RUSK *and the*
MIT SCRATCH TEAM
DECEMBER 2016, 75 CARDS, $24.95
ISBN 978-1-59327-774-1
full color, box set

LEARN TO PROGRAM WITH SCRATCH

A Visual Introduction to Programming with Games, Art, Science, and Math

by MAJED MARJI
FEBRUARY 2014, 288 PP., $34.95
ISBN 978-1-59327-543-3
full color

PYTHON FOR KIDS

A Playful Introduction to Programming

by JASON R. BRIGGS
DECEMBER 2012, 344 PP., $34.95
ISBN 978-1-59327-407-8
full color

1.800.420.7240 or 1.415.863.9900 | sales@nostarch.com | www.nostarch.com